Praise for *Culture Ignited*

Jason Richmond has done it again! *Culture Ignited*, coauthored with Jeanne Kerr and Malcolm Nicholl, is a superb follow-up to *Culture Spark*, diving deeper into how we shape our organization's culture to thrive. In a post-pandemic world, every corporate leader will find dynamic, actionable information in the five disciplines. Well researched and highly readable.

Marshall Goldsmith, *Thinkers50* #1 Executive Coach for 10 years and *New York Times* #1 bestselling author of *Triggers, Mojo,* and *What Got You Here Won't Get You There*

Congratulations to Jason, Jeanne, and Malcolm for a timely, thoughtful, and practical book aimed at better workplaces, stronger cultures, and improved performance. These are difficult goals under any circumstance, let alone in these turbulent and uncertain times. I particularly liked the way the authors synthesized the latest relevant research and blended it with their own insights and advice. The result is a very useful and usable contribution.

David C. Forman, bestselling author of *Fearless Talent Choice* and Adjunct Professor, Pepperdine University

Culture Ignited gives leaders so many useful strategies that are practical and easy to understand, and which are sure to have a positive impact on the workplace. A must-read as organizations struggle to regain their footing and ignite their culture following any crisis.

Hanlie van Wyk, coauthor of *The 11th Habit: Design Your Company Culture to Foster the Habits of High Performance*

Companies with adaptive leadership that responded quickly and thoughtfully to the coronavirus pandemic transformed their businesses for long-term success by becoming more agile. Sometimes necessity is the mother of invention. The key now is to not revert to type and keep going on the transformation journey of enterprise agility. Jason Richmond has analyzed the performance of major corporations and devised an important five-discipline template for any senior leader to follow.

Mike Richardson, CEO/President and
Enterprise Agility Thought Leader

Great culture is a critical element of organizational success, most especially when leading in disruptive times. Jason Richmond's *Culture Ignited* shares strategies and actions that can help leaders guide their teams through chaos while nurturing a dynamic and engaging culture. A must-read for leaders wanting to build a thriving organizational culture.

Mahan Tavakoli, CEO, Strategic Leadership Ventures
and host Partnering Leadership podcast

CULTURE IGNITED

5 Disciplines for Adaptive Leadership

CULTURE
IGNITED

5 Disciplines for Adaptive Leadership

JASON RICHMOND
with Jeanne Kerr and Malcolm J. Nicholl

Ideal Outcomes, Inc.
Colorado Springs, Colorado

To the memory of John Covilli—mentor, coach, guide,
a source of inspiration, and great friend. RIP.
– Jason Richmond

Culture Ignited: 5 Disciplines for Adaptive Leadership
Jason Richmond with Jeanne Kerr and Malcolm J. Nicholl

Ideal Outcomes, Inc.
Colorado Springs, Colorado
https://idealoutcomesinc.com
contact@idealoutcomesinc.com

ISBN: 978-1-7337105-4-1 (soft cover)
ISBN: 978-1-7337105-5-8 (eBook)
ISBN: 978-1-7337105-6-5 (Audiobook)

Library of Congress Control Number: 2021915440

Edited by Melanie Mulhall, Dragonheart
Cover design by Nicholas Schmitt
Interior layout by Nick Zelinger, NZ Graphics

About the cover: There's much to be admired in the chameleon. Famed for its remarkable ability to change color, the chameleon epitomizes adaptive behavior. With a history that dates back millions of years, it has lived through numerous crises and survived. It can see better than other animals with eyes that provide a full 360-degree arc of vision.

First Edition

Printed in the United States of America

Contents

FREE eBook!

As a thank-you for purchasing *Culture Ignited,*
we'd like to give you a complimentary
copy of Jason Richmond's first book *Culture Spark.*
Praised as "the definitive guide to developing
a winning culture," this 210-page
eBook is yours 100% **FREE.**
A $9.99 value.
Email your request with your full name to:
contact@idealoutcomesinc.com.

Foreword

I met Jason Richmond for the first time when he interviewed me for his book *Culture Spark: 5 Steps to Ignite and Sustain Organizational Growth*. At that time, I was vice president of human resources for a national financial services organization where I headed talent management, training and development, analytics, and human resources information systems. I was also an adjunct professor at the University of Pennsylvania where I still continue to teach a graduate level course on human capital leadership.

Upon meeting Jason, I immediately felt I had met a kindred spirit, someone who has a very strong desire, like me, to help leaders shape their organization's culture and create great places for people to work. *Culture Spark* was published in 2019 to great acclaim. I believe it was so well-received because it is a "practitioner's" book. It's loaded with practical advice, common sense notions of leadership, and easy to understand concepts, models, and ideas that are immediately accessible and relatable to the challenges of leading in today's ever-changing business world.

Jason's newest book *Culture Ignited: 5 Disciplines for Adaptive Leadership*, carries on the tradition of being immensely practical and accessible for leaders. This time, however, Jason incorporates critical lessons and insights that he and those he interviewed for the book have learned from working and leading in the age of the global pandemic. These lessons roll up into five key leadership disciplines: Inspire and communicate a shared purpose. Build trust and authenticity. Hone your performance management skills. Build capability and develop your talent. Create belonging through diversity and inclusion.

I believe that the five disciplines provide leaders with the essential insights, experience, and business skills they will need to learn and apply truly to reset the culture of their organization and prepare it for the post-pandemic era.

To make *Culture Ignited* even more accessible, Jason adeptly weaves together all the wisdom and all the lessons he has learned and channels them through the character of Susan, a mid-level manager of a customer operations team. We follow Susan's journey over a year of the pandemic by reading her diary entries as she reflects on her experience as a leader and tells her own leadership story. By the end, we see how Susan learns quickly to adapt to new ways of working in turbulent and uncertain times and how she prepares herself, her people, and her organization for the next crisis that will inevitably come.

I am immensely grateful to Jason and his team at Ideal Outcomes for their significant contribution to the field of leadership development. It is a great honor for me to be associated with Jason's work. I am excited to share the book with my students and clients, and I look forward to integrating its valuable lessons into my own leadership practice, coaching, and teaching.

Stephen G. Hart
Senior Consultant and Executive Coach
The Professional Development Group, LLC
August 2021

Introduction

The COVID-19 pandemic challenged corporate leaders in ways they were never challenged before. It was a once-in-a-century catastrophe that changed the business world forever, a global seismic shake-up. It was also one that inspired renewed agility, innovation, and teamwork.

Most of all, it served as a wake-up call, making us more aware than ever of the need for corporate leaders to prepare for *any* kind of crisis, to have a management plan in place, and to act quickly, decisively, and with empathy when the next crisis strikes. And there *will* be a next crisis. There always is.

As culture change strategists during *this* crisis, we researched best practices and trends, evaluated new authoritative surveys, studies, and academic analyses, and picked the brains of hands-on thought leaders. Navigating the turbulence of the pandemic was a learning experience that few leaders anticipated, and it will have long-term ramifications for the way companies operate.

How can you and your organization be better prepared to face the next unimagined crisis? How can your corporate culture be maintained? What attributes will help senior leaders work their way through all aspects of the challenge? How will you recruit, hire, onboard, communicate, and train during tumultuous times?

In this book, we have distilled what we know—from our own experiences and from those of notable corporate leaders—into a step-by-step road map founded on five disciplines:

1. Inspire and communicate a shared purpose.
2. Build trust and authenticity.
3. Hone your performance management skills.
4. Build capability and develop your talent.
5. Create belonging through diversity and inclusion.

We address the critical role of senior leaders and explore how a crisis can be turned into opportunity. Our goal is to equip and empower executives, enabling them to successfully lead an organization to overcome challenges never taught in business school.

This work continues the message and advice in Jason's previous book, *Culture Spark: 5 Steps to Ignite and Sustain Organizational Growth.* Sustain is a key word because the impact of 2020 and 2021 has far-reaching consequences. Companies with adaptive leadership that responded quickly and thoughtfully made sustainable transformations for long-haul success. They ignited their culture. Working hand in glove with these leaders in major corporations has led us to the five-discipline template for *your* success.

1

From Shock to Coping

"Office centricity is over."
—Tobi Lütke, CEO, Shopify

Day One

I can't believe it. Half of what I need is still at the office. They gave me less than an hour to pack up my files, gather my books, and grab my laptop. Thank God I have a laptop. I have no idea what the folks in customer service are going to do. And I bet IT is going insane.

Yesterday I was doing my one-hour slog on the freeway, listening to the news, and sipping a latte. And now I'm at home trying to get this VPN thing to work. And my coffee tastes like dishwater.

Okay, so we're using Zoom. Great. I finally get WebEx to work and they tell us to download this other platform. Works better with video, they say. Video! Crap. My office is a mess. The kids' projects are all over my desk, and I wonder if they can see all the cat hair. This is so embarrassing. I'm working from home, but I can't even stay in my sweats. And I have to go on camera without looking like I just got out of bed. I'm working from home but still have to put on lipstick. Who would have thought?

Meet Susan, a mid-level manager of a customer operations team whose experiences during 2020 and 2021 may have been much like yours. We will follow her journey, sharing her thoughts and words, as we develop the strategies and actions designed to take you out of chaos and toward a dynamic, engaging organizational environment and culture.

Finding Ways to Cope

There had been a trend toward remote work in the US before the pandemic. Some 4.7 million employees worked from home at least half of the time—just 3.4 percent of the workforce—but a much greater number, at least 62 percent, occasionally worked remotely.[1, 2]

Almost Overnight, Companies Changed Everything

During the first phase of the pandemic, most companies scrambled to implement remote strategies, and many employees either learned how to manage it hands-on or received quick and dirty training, which was reflected in a huge uptick in videoconferencing:

- Usage of Zoom soared more than 300 percent.

- Cisco's WebEx hosted more than 20 billion meetings in April 2020, compared with 14 billion in March and 7 billion in February.

- Microsoft Teams saw more than 200 million participants generate four billion meeting minutes in a single day.

Microsoft CEO Satya Nadella said, "We've seen two years' worth of digital transformation in two months."[3]

Tech companies readily embraced the change. Twitter said their employees had the option of *never* returning to work in their office. Slack Technologies foresaw anywhere from 20 percent to 40 percent of its employees continuing to work remotely. Dropbox went a step further and envisioned workers only going into their offices for collaboration days.

Shopify CEO Tobi Lütke reflected the thinking of many leaders when he said, "Office centricity is over."

Productivity Was Surprisingly High

One of management's biggest fears has been that remote work would lead to inefficiencies and lower productivity. Not so, according to our own experiences and most research.

Through cloud-based business tools, chat applications, and email, workplace-monitoring firm Prodoscore analyzed data points from thirty thousand Americans and concluded that workers were 47 percent more productive in March and April of 2020 than the same two months the previous year.[4]

Companies Gained Cost Savings

Increased productivity translates into cost savings. Corporate overhead is also reduced when there's less need for office space and all its attendant expenses—utilities, maintenance, cafeteria, and so forth. Companies also reduce costs when corporate travel slams to a halt.

How Do Employees React?

According to a Gallup survey, as the pandemic eased, 23 percent of workers said they'd prefer working from home always or sometimes, which was considerably more than before COVID-19 struck.[5] Top motivators for employees include an improved work-life balance and the elimination of commute time. They also enjoy fewer interruptions and more time to focus on the tasks at hand.

In the early months of the pandemic, a survey by virtual private network (VPN) service provider NordVPN, which tracks when users are connected to its service, found that homebound employees in the US logged a staggering three hours more per day than they had before they were homebound.[6]

Does Not Having to Commute Make a Difference?

Once freed from a long commute, many employees relish the extra time acquired, money saved on transportation, and freedom from the daily hassle. Commuting can be very stressful. The Ford European Commuter Survey of more than 5,500 commuters in six major cities found that "the journey to work causes more stress than their actual jobs (or even the dentist)."[7]

On the other hand, while commutes are rated one of the most stressful and undesirable parts of the day, the *Harvard Business Review* made an interesting observation: Having no commute at all is not without its problems, and one of them is separating work life from personal life. "Instead of shutting down the computer and rattling home on a crowded train at 6:00 p.m., many people are working later than ever, 'just one more email' stretching into an extra two hours hunched over the laptop."[8]

Unplugging is not a new problem for remote workers. Putting in more time corresponds with pre-pandemic studies of remote workers in which 23 percent reported working longer hours and 22 percent said that unplugging was their biggest struggle. These two issues are worth bearing in mind for managers who harbor lingering doubts about the work ethic of out-of-sight employees.

Remote work was forced upon most workers in a rushed, less-than-perfect manner while they struggled to handle other pandemic-related issues. But now that the genie is out of the bottle and they have appreciated its benefits, that genie is not going to vanish back inside.

As Korn Ferry CEO Gary Burnison said, "To thrive, all companies will need to think and act like startups by reimagining their future. If they don't, their competition will. Why? Because in the next two years we will see more changes than we've seen in the last twenty. And that change must bubble up from within an organization, not merely cascade down."

This means that an essential element for the implementation of a successful work-from-home program is learning how to communicate and work effectively to maintain productivity, and especially to maintain company culture. Managers must keep in touch as closely as if their teams were just down the corridor. It can be done. It has been done.

Day Five

I need to stop snacking so much. It's not a substitute for getting up and poking my head into my folks' offices. I'm going to gain a ton of weight, and they say the camera adds ten pounds. OMG! Three Zoom meetings today. I swear we're having more meetings now than when we were in the office.

And I need to get my arms around what my people are doing. I just know Danny is spending time in his workshop. I haven't seen an email from him in two days. I can't take anyone to lunch. I miss my walks with my coworkers. We were having great conversations and getting exercise at the same time. Every time we have a Zoom call, Mary says her connection is bad and she has to drop off. Yeah, right. So why does it take her forever to call back in by phone? This is exhausting.

Make It Work

Companies that may have been reluctant to invest in the technological infrastructure required for large-scale remote work had no choice but to do so. Remote work is not only here to stay, it will expand.

A remote work program requires several ingredients for success, so let's look at some best practices you can deploy for your organization.

The Right Tools

A fundamental requirement for working remotely is to make sure everyone has a stable, fast, and secure internet connection. To ensure continuity, partner with your IT teams and have them determine that the right software is in place for VPN and team collaboration tools like Zoom, Slack, and WebEx.

Cybersecurity is paramount. With so many employees working remotely and connecting online via numerous platforms, the vulnerability to being hacked is greatly increased. Your employees must have the right security software, both from a network perspective and on their individual devices. Maintaining data integrity and the privacy of critical business documents is less costly than dealing with a serious data breach.

What else can you do to reduce the risk? The Cyber Management Alliance, one of the global frontrunners in cyber crisis management, has created a "Remote Working Cybersecurity checklist."[9] Their suggestions range from the obvious requirement of password protection to extra precautions when using mobile devices. One message in particular struck home to us: Create a culture where employees aren't afraid to own up to making a mistake. If they click on a malicious link, for instance, it's important they let you know about it before it evolves into a widespread attack.

Build in Social Time

When workers are remote, we lose that impromptu chat in the breakroom or by the coffee pot. And when this kind of naturally occurring socialization is lost, we need to purposely create it. Loneliness is a pervasive and growing problem according to The Society for Human Resources (SHRM), particularly with Generation Z (18- to 24-year-olds) as well as Millennials.[10]

Managers can set reminders on their calendars to call each team member at least once a week, just to touch base. After all, when you walk by someone's cubicle or office, you usually take a few minutes to chat. With remote workers, such spontaneous interactions must be replaced with purposeful action. Some employees feel very isolated with remote work. Ask staff—individually and directly—how they feel about being remote.

Find time to have fun, and get creative. If celebrating birthdays is a tradition, sing happy birthday during a virtual meeting or during one of your regular one-on-one calls. Maybe hold a virtual lunch and recipe exchange where people share recipes online and use their computer camera or phones to show the food they are eating. Or have a meet-and-greet with employees' pets. You could also get your team to share new hobbies or other activities they have started enjoying. All of this creates camaraderie and trust, as well as providing comfort for those under stress.

Set Boundaries and Guidelines

First, establish some structure. This is especially important if employees are working from home for the first time. Make sure they know productivity expectations by setting weekly and monthly goals together, and discuss progress at least biweekly. Have a clear agenda for each call and distribute it ahead of time so those uncomfortable about speaking up can prepare and be more willing to make their voices heard. Try to get everyone's voice "into the room" at least once.

Allow for open discussion about projects and incorporate time for brainstorming and problem-solving. Give people the opportunity to ask for help—and provide it. Don't forget to congratulate team members who have made special contributions.

For the benefit of employees who prefer to absorb information through text, you might host video meetings with closed captioning. Technology also exists for transcribing as well as recording online meetings. Recorded meetings are great for those who prefer to get information by auditory means and want to review the meeting later, while transcribed meetings are good for those who prefer to read rather than listen. Both ensure full transparency.

Finally, don't micromanage your employees. Trust that they will get their work done. If you have structured discussions each week, you will quickly discover if they struggle with working from home.

Ask employees to write up a summary of each of these conversations, including accomplishments, next steps, commitments, and deadlines. If your company uses Office 365, OneNote is a useful tool to track these meetings.

Healthy Work Habits

When it comes to remote working, make sure your staff understands that the company's need for productivity must be balanced with their need for quality time for themselves.

In a pre-pandemic survey, 59 percent of workers admitted that they checked in with their bosses or coworkers at least once a day *while on vacation*, and 23 percent did so three times a day.[11] Such behavior is not conducive to you or your employees' mental health or to a healthy company culture. Everyone needs downtime, and such behavior sends the message that downtime (and family life) are not respected.

Clearly, the stress of working from home, an increased reliance on virtual connectivity, and the potential for working longer hours all raise the risk of burnout. Balance is critical. It's important for leaders to take the lead and encourage more healthy work habits such as the following:

- Managing technology: Urge your people to avoid becoming slaves to technology, obsessively checking email at all hours of the day and night because home has become the office. Model healthy habits. Even if you must draft emails in the evening or on weekends, instead of sending them out, save them in drafts to be delivered during normal work time. Do not check in when you are on vacation and tell employees you do not expect them to do so either.

- Video scramble: Be aware that split-second delays in video transmission can be unsettling, and video cannot replicate the intimacy and importance of in-person communication. Thalia Wheatley, a professor of psychological and brain science at Dartmouth who studies the difference between face-to-face and online interaction, told *Time* magazine, "Screens are distancing. In face-to-face communication, you are sharing a moment in time and space with someone. That is incredibly compelling for our ancient brains."[12]

- Encourage employees to pretend their remote location is the office: Rolling out of bed, grabbing a cup of coffee, and not changing out of their pajamas may seem like a treat, but it doesn't create a "working" mindset.

- Keep office hours: Suggest that employees try to maintain a similar schedule to the one they had at the company offices. Among other things, that means encouraging them to take as many—or more—breaks as they took at the office. Text employees once in a while to remind them to get up and move or stretch. Keep this light and humorous to generate maximum motivation. You don't want to sound like a drill sergeant.

As we have seen, remote work is not going to be a fleeting crisis phenomenon. Organizations have recognized it is here to stay, and they need to carefully consider not only how to make it work, but also when it is appropriate to ask employees to come to the office. Executives may be anxious to restore office work, but many employees are in no hurry. Companies need to develop strategies that align organizational goals with employee needs and expectations for flexibility and safety.

2

Inspire and Communicate a Shared Purpose

"There are decades where nothing happens and there are weeks where decades happen."
—Vladimir Lenin

1 — **Shared Purpose** | 2 — Trust & Authenticity | 3 — Performance Management | 4 — Talent Development | 5 — Diversity & Inclusion

Day Ten

Okay, it's been two weeks. Zoom is getting a bit easier, and I finally have a bit of a system to my day. The kids are doing their homework (I think), and thankfully, my husband has figured out that I cannot be the only homework monitor. It still all feels unreal though. We're plugging the dike and heading off major disasters, but I feel so disconnected. What's going on with our customers? We were building a new purchasing platform, but do customers even still want our products? How can we serve them without seeing them? Nothing is as it was, and I'm really struggling with my role and priorities. I went from face-to-face customer visits and walk-throughs of their premises to this. And overnight! Somehow, we need to move from reacting to everything to planning and coordinating again. But where do we start? And if I'm feeling this way, how is my team feeling?

"Corporate culture encompasses how we share information and communicate with one another, how we treat people, how we make decisions, the kinds of polices (or lack of policies) we have, and how we are structured. Culture changes and evolves. In fact, it *needs* to change and evolve." That was how Jason Richmond defined corporate culture in his previous book, *Culture Spark: 5 Steps to Ignite and Sustain Organizational Growth*. And the need for culture to change and evolve is more relevant now than ever.

While companies rushed to set up systems to handle remote work and CFOs juggled finances to stay afloat, it would have been easy to concentrate on survival and push corporate culture aside. But a crisis brings into sharp focus the value of a strong culture to organizational success. At the same time, it allows employees to see if their corporate culture stands up to the test.

"Driving culture change" ranks in the top three leadership development priorities, according to a global Korn Ferry study.[13] Yet 72 percent of corporate leaders admit their organizations struggle to get their culture right.

Sometimes it takes a crisis to force change and make senior executives rethink everything about the way they operate. A dramatic, out-of-the-blue, once-in-a-lifetime event sparks radical reflection on improvements that must be made, and leaders must be open to radical change. "What can we do better?" is an important question for organizations to ask the right people—constantly. Include a cross section of departments, corporate disciplines, roles, levels, and responsibilities. It is not enough to ask managers what their people think. The perspective must come from individual experience. Holding conversations of this kind are greatly appreciated by the workforce and create a higher level of employee engagement, especially when employees see their suggestions adopted.

When leaders do not ask this question, they create a culture of compliance rather than a culture of cooperation. Employees may continue to do their jobs and fulfill requirements enough to earn their paycheck, but engagement will drop and they won't expend that extra level of effort required to enhance performance. Over time, performance will flatline, talent will be harder to retain, and creativity and innovation will suffer. And to drive improvements in customer retention, product and service quality, and growth, discussions must also occur with other stakeholders: customers, suppliers, and strategic partners.

There's no doubt that the sudden stress of the lockdown during the recent pandemic put unimaginable pressures on culture, which is the heart and soul of your organization and needs to be nourished.[14] The crisis highlighted the fact that a company's culture and the people who comprise that culture matter more than ever, and the foundation for a healthy culture is a compelling purpose around which its workers rally.

Companies with a healthy culture thrive because they create the sense that everyone is in it together. Those companies also care about more than the bottom line. Making a profit is essential, certainly, but purpose is what drives commitment and passion. Purpose is what differentiates you to your customers, vendors, employees, and potential employees.

The flourishing businesses will be those whose leaders recognize that purpose drives profits and profits sustain purpose. They go hand in hand. Purpose-driven business metrics can help you determine how much impact you have on the company, organization, society, and/or community you seek to influence. Examples of purpose-driven metrics that truly differentiate you from the competition include:

- Brand loyalty,
- Quality job applicants from employee referrals,
- Community involvement,
- Retention of employees, particularly high performers,
- Customer retention, repeat business, customer referrals, and
- Product/service innovation.

Day Fifteen

That was a great meeting. Listening to our CEO and my director explain their shared vision made a huge difference in my mind. I wish they had done that a week sooner, but I understand that they were trying to get their arms around everything, just like me.

I'm also excited that we will be continuing these conversations in every department. Not only are they giving us great direction, they want our ideas to develop the plan! I need to make sure my team understands that although it isn't business as usual—and may never be again—our customers are still our focus and priority. I should put together a brainstorming session with the team to find out what they think is important to do about that. They talk to customers every day.

To start, I'm going to write up what I think the top three challenges for our accounts in the present working environment are and send it out to my team. I'll ask them to add to what I send them and make a list of approaches to meet our customers' needs. If our customers see us being proactive, they're going to have confidence in us. I think what is most important is to make sure everyone on the team is on board and contributes. If I've been feeling disconnected, they must be too. It's my job to reconnect them to what our company is all about.

Maintaining and Strengthening Culture in Tough Times

As our manager Susan realized, not only do leaders need to maintain culture in challenging times, they also need to implement strategies to strengthen and secure culture for the long-term.

Revisit and Reinforce Your Purpose

When everyone is together under the same roof, it's much easier to instill a sense of shared purpose and build a team of like-minded individuals. With some effort and creativity, leaders can develop a *virtual* sense of camaraderie.

Leaders need to lead by example and not only reiterate the corporate purpose but also live it and display it in every action they take. A pre-pandemic Deloitte report, "Global Human Capital Trends," revealed that employees desired purpose and meaning more than money.[15] They were more interested in their company's contribution to the world than the bottom line. The emergence of purpose as a driving force is particularly compelling, given its overarching impact on all aspects of work and business. A sense of purpose can help employees navigate high levels of uncertainty and change and ensure that their efforts are quickly aligned with the highest-value activities.

McKinsey research showed that survey respondents "living their purpose" at work had four times higher engagement and five times higher well-being and stated, "Purpose above all else, enables forthright decision-making at speed."[16] Deloitte, in its "2020 Global Human Capital Trends" report, put it this way: "To strengthen the link between belonging and organizational performance, organizations need to do more than treat their workers fairly and respectfully; they must enable a deeper connection by drawing visible linkages as to how their contributions are making an impact on the organization and society as a whole."

Out of Sight but Not Out of Mind

Maintaining your corporate culture while managing a remote workforce is no small undertaking. As Tracy Brower, author of *Bringing Life to Work: A Guide for Leaders and Organizations*, says, "A culture is significantly shaped by the worst behavior it will tolerate." What's unique about the pandemic is it may be harder to see and be aware of employee choices and actions which may make it harder to validate the behaviors you want.[17]

It is clearly time to ramp up the frequency and quality of your communication. One email will not get the job done. Change will continue to unfold at breakneck speed, which requires communication to be brief and frequent.

Emphasize Positive Change

Nothing drives desired behavior like positive reinforcement. Enable a way for employees to share success stories that are directly tied to your stated purpose and your values. When employees see how their actions relate to the bigger picture, they connect the dots and understand where to invest their energy. Tap into customers for success stories as well. These kinds of actions reinforce your commitment to your purpose and inspire loyalty from employees and customers alike.

Reimagine the Employee Experience

During the pandemic, many organizations had to reinvent processes and workflows that had been designed for a brick-and-mortar environment, quickly and with minimal thought to the design or effectiveness of those remedial solutions. Now is the time to honestly evaluate what works and what doesn't work. What obstacles exist to living your purpose? What workflows impede good service or a positive employee experience? What barriers to moving forward are related to technology that is not conducive to new ways of doing business? Purposeful work is satisfying, and such satisfaction drives engagement and commitment.

Create a Positive Working Environment

Go beyond work-life balance. Look for ways to create the sense for employees that their jobs do not feel like work. Empower employees. Give them flexibility and autonomy while challenging them to achieve more and contribute to the organization's purpose. If you develop an environment with these attributes and acknowledge employees for their contributions, you develop an enduring culture.

Crises stretch senior executives to an unimageable extent, but real leaders can turn unprecedented challenges into ways to stimulate and strengthen corporate culture and reignite employees' belief in the business for an even brighter future.

3

Build Trust
and Authenticity

"Culture helps guide organizations during times of change, and there is no better test for the strength of your culture than a challenging, chaotic and uncertain time."

—Gallup

Two Months

Looks like this is not going away any time soon. I really do miss being in the office. Even my commute had its positives. At least when I got home, I was home! The commute gave me some closure to the day. Now it feels like the hours run together.

I know I'm not alone in feeling this way. I can't believe that my boss called me the other day and commented on the emails I've been sending in the evenings. She actually asked me to stop doing that! I have to admit, this is the first time a boss has told me to stop working so much. She even said that we're both setting a bad example for our employees and need to stop working so many hours. It made me feel a lot better to hear that she also feels she's working 24/7. She was always the person to respect and even encourage hard work and long hours. Something has changed.

In my next team call, I'm going to tell my team about that conversation and ask them what they think and how they're feeling. Funny, I always thought we were a pretty honest company, but this is a shift in a new direction. And I like it.

A sudden swing to remote work may have highlighted culture issues that were hidden or not as impactful in an office setting. The way in which these issues reveal themselves varies but often include how employees take care of customers or treat each other. The key is to make culture a priority. Recognize that it is going to take consistent focus and effort and that empathetic and transparent leadership is a significant requirement to build or rebuild your culture, no matter how difficult or painful it is to implement.

We all know the negative impact of the rumor mill, and when people are spread out and working from home, picking up on and dispelling rumors can be particularly challenging—all the more reason to lay the foundation for trust and authenticity through clear, consistent communication. It may sound contradictory, but to achieve authenticity takes careful planning to decide what you are going to say, how you will say it, and how often you will communicate. Occasional emails are not going to cut it.

Build Trust through Communication

Step up your communication to your workforce. Frequent updates with open and forthright progress reports from the top are essential. Use one or more platforms for those communications, including email blasts, audio-video conferencing, and online town halls. Employees are eager to hear from their corporate leaders.

The 2021 Edelman Trust Barometer, a global survey of more than thirty thousand people, found that communication from "my employer" was the most trusted source of communication (61 percent), beating out national government (58 percent), traditional media (57 percent), and social media (39 percent.)[18] Take advantage of that confidence and continuously look for ways to generate and sustain trust with your workforce.

Trust is the foundation upon which relationships are built, and it's a two-way street. Research shows that when workers are trusted by their managers, they are much more likely to reciprocate that trust.[19] In turn, they will perform to a greater extent at a higher level and exceed expectations. Go out of your way to deliberately signal your trust. Don't *assume* your employees know that you trust them. They're not mind readers, so you have to tell them.

Encourage feedback, and be responsive both on an individual basis and through company-wide communications. Strive not only to be positive and uplifting, but also to be honest and realistic.

Hold live question-and-answer sessions during which employees can ask senior management anything or set up an online link for employees to pose questions to senior leadership twenty-four hours a day. You may find that employees who were too shy to interact publicly are more inclined to participate in a private medium. If you cannot answer some questions on the spot, provide answers in the next team or company-wide communication.

Constantly embed purpose in how you communicate with your employees, and when you implement business changes, always link them with your purpose. An effective approach is to provide real-world examples of how purpose is cultivated by members of your organization. Share stories of these role models at every opportunity and continue to keep a focus on long-term cultural priorities through regular contact.

One of our clients, a global manufacturer, promotes company purpose through seven cultural pillars that clearly describe why they exist. Their learning and development program, which we created, includes a commitment to develop more than six hundred middle managers in the next three years, based on those seven pillars. One of the chief goals is to ensure a consistent understanding of the pillars and enable managers to forge the skills and competencies to consistently communicate them and model key behaviors.

For another client, a large public utility, the paramount issue—both for employees and the public—is safety. The company ensures communication of purpose by starting every meeting, whether an executive session or skills-based training for union employees, with a message about safety. The company never misses the opportunity to remind everyone of this mission-critical focus.

Build Trust through Empathy

Leaders should respond and act with empathy, displaying a genuine understanding of the difficulties their employees have endured. You can't pay lip service to this need. It's an essential part of leadership in a crisis.

Show your team that you care about them on a personal level and not simply because they get their work done. This requires frequently asking people in private how they are doing and what they need, coupled with listening sincerely and attentively to their responses. Don't take it at face value if they consistently maintain that they are fine. Probe a bit. Confide an issue with which you struggle and inquire how they are dealing with the same challenges. This gives them permission to express concerns. Make sure they understand how they fit in the greater scheme of things, and take responsibility for showing them that they're not just a name on a paycheck.

Build Trust through Flexibility

Don't feel compelled to check in with employees working remotely all day, every day because they're not within sight to confirm that they are working. Trust that they are. Don't worry so much about the hours they're working.

As mentioned earlier, studies show many are actually working longer hours than when they worked at the office. Instead of checking up on them, concentrate on results and accomplishments. How productive are they? Most workers respond positively to freedom, and no one likes to be micromanaged. Trust your team to do their jobs.

When employees work from home and are out of sight, it's inevitable that managers wonder how much time is spent on work rather than doing household chores or other personal activities. Some companies respond by installing various kinds of computer surveillance such as keystroke capture or even video links. That's not such a good idea. One survey discovered that 49 percent of employees subjected to stringent monitoring reported severe anxiety as a result of such obvious lack of trust.[20]

Give your team members flexibility, especially since working from home can involve domestic conflicts because spouses and kids have their own schedules. If you trust employees to juggle their workload with their family responsibilities, they will respond accordingly and contribute to the overall success of the company.

Flexibility is not just about work schedules. Flexibility needs to be embedded in all aspects of the work environment, and it means having confidence in your own leadership skills and an open, inclusive mindset that includes inviting new ideas, encouraging innovation and experimentation, and adopting new processes. This requires you to build your ability to empower your teams and to think differently about how you delegate projects and assignments. It also means helping your teams cultivate their own support networks so you are not the only person they rely on for guidance and direction.

Reach Out in New Ways

The pandemic gave companies the opportunity to connect in ways they would otherwise never have been forced to consider. For example, Axonify, a leading frontline employee training firm, launched its own virtual talk show.[21] Hosted by the company's chief learning architect, it featured employees, and it sparked new ideas and much-needed laughter.

Salesforce created an online talent show with entries from more than 500 employees. The finale, hosted by *Saturday Night Live* comedian, Colin Jost, included a live performance from Jewel and was judged by four Salesforce executives in humorous attire.[22] Peerfit, a digital fitness company, built camaraderie with a virtual water cooler channel on its internal messaging platform as well as channels where employees could post photos of their pets and discuss what they were binge-watching. Other strategies include fun-based activities such as virtual game tournaments, photo competitions depicting working from home, and daily virtual coffee breaks.[23]

Ultimate Medical Academy, a nonprofit healthcare educational institution, snail mailed motivational posters to its employees that used its mascot, Journey the Puma, and became a common home office backdrop during its video calls. In a time when digital communication has become dominant, you can use snail mail to great advantage. Receiving a gift card in a stamped envelope in your home mailbox is a pleasant surprise. So are handwritten thank-you notes.[24]

Be a Coach, Not a Boss

Sometimes it is more important to be a coach than a boss. And a critical element of good coaching is asking the right questions. In general, ask more and tell less. You can create ownership and commitment by gleaning employees' ideas on how to solve problems. Provide direction, define broad expectations, and get out of the way except when providing important feedback.

Having led the New England Patriots to a record six Super Bowl championships, Bill Belichick is much admired in the NFL world for his coaching skills. How well would the Patriots continue to perform if he gave formal feedback to his players only once or twice a season?

Yet this is how most businesses manage performance. They set annual and often meaningless goals that frequently change but are rarely revisited. Managers do a poor job of providing constructive or negative feedback. Sadly, they also struggle to give praise, and they do not know how to develop, coach, or course-correct employees.

Rethinking how we manage performance is long overdue. A simple shift in perspective to *leading* performance rather than just *managing* performance lays the foundation for a more inspirational, motivational approach. Leading implies empowerment and autonomy for employees and a manager who is a coach to team members rather than a top-down boss.

Gallup research shows a connection between coaching and creativity, largely because coaches establish relationships that provide a safe platform for conceptualizing and offering ideas. Coaches are more likely to accept, not forgive, mistakes. Taking risks and possibly making mistakes are part of finding new and better solutions. As a result of the pandemic, managers have had to become more available, more communicative, and more open than ever before, leading to a huge improvement in team engagement. Such bosses demonstrate leadership agility and ignite their cultures in powerful ways.

Take Advantage of Culture Committees

We've long advocated instituting culture committees within companies. They are a powerful way to involve many levels of employees and multiple locations in building an organic culture and ensuring that it is shared across regions and sustained as the company grows.

It is important to recognize the value offered by these committees. They should be developed and treated as important cultural influencers and not simply be considered token employee task forces. How you establish a culture committee is vital. Focus them on being action oriented. Empower them to implement culture chat boards and other communication platforms. Make sure membership is diverse and representative of all employee perspectives. Include an executive in the team to facilitate communication with senior leaders, and rotate participants yearly to ensure fresh ideas and a broad opportunity to contribute.

Some organizations have seen fit to form culture *continuity* committees. Having a culture continuity plan in times of crisis is just as important as having a business continuity plan. As an example, Ultimate Medical Academy's vice president of admissions, Steve Hernandez, says, "The situation [pandemic] required us to examine the traditions and values that define our culture, and we realized it's not about where we're located; it's about what we value, how we support each other and why we do what we do. By emphasizing culture continuity, we have maintained the core functions of our institution in ways that celebrate our mission, values, and people."[25]

Authenticity Founded in Transparency

Transparency is tough for many organizations and for many leaders. Many of us were taught that being a leader meant knowing all the answers and have worked in environments where making a mistake was tantamount to career disaster.

The reality is that we cannot reignite our culture without first acknowledging the current state—which is likely to have created issues—when a crisis occurs. If we are not candid about these issues, the rumor mill will run rampant, as will mistrust. Trust is fragile, easily broken, and hard to regain.

Leaders need to take a long, hard look inward and ask themselves if they are part of the problem. No culture can sustain itself without authenticity and emotional intelligence. Can you see things from your employees' point of view? Are you a role model for managing stress in challenging times? Do you demonstrate resiliency and the ability to lead with minimal conflict and maximum collaboration?

Transparency does not mean sharing information that cannot be shared or violating confidentiality. There are occasions when you have to tell employees, "I cannot answer that question at this time." But you do not have to leave it at that. Tell them what you can tell them, even if it's nothing more than an acknowledgment that the subject in question is currently being discussed. It is fine to say there is no new information and that you will communicate what you can as soon as you can.

If issues are common knowledge, don't try to tap dance or deflect, and do not get defensive. People quickly see through those things, and your credibility, along with their trust in you, go right out the window. Acknowledge challenges and offset them with what you plan to do about them. In other words, be authentic by being transparent and accountable. Here are a few examples:

- Yes, our gender pay gap is X%. We have a plan to eliminate it over Y years and will report on progress.

- Yes, our type of business uses lots of water. It is a challenge throughout our industry. Our goal is to reduce it by X percent over the next three years, and this is what we are doing to reduce our consumption.

- Yes, our diversity record is poor. Here is what we are doing to address that.

- Yes, we made mistakes in our rush to bring people back into the office. We now have a task force of employees and managers working on a better strategy. Would you be interested in participating?

This combination of purpose, commitment, transparency, and authenticity fosters two things that all leaders should be seeking to develop and retain: trust and confidence.

Thomas Jefferson once said, "Honesty is the first chapter in the book of wisdom." When leaders remove their masks, when they are willing to risk losing face, and when they show their genuineness to their people, they create lasting trust and connections. And their people return the favor in kind with passion, engagement, and loyalty. Physical proximity with your employees may not always be possible, but mental and emotional proximity always is.

4

Hone Your Performance Management Skills

"It is difficult to have a highly competitive organization without highly competitive talent."

—Pearl Zhu, author, *Performance Master: Take a Holistic Approach to Unlock Digital Performance*

Five Months

Reflecting back on the last five months has been interesting. I'm astonished by how much we're accomplishing. I know I was micromanaging at first because I thought that if I couldn't see people working, I wouldn't be able to tell if they were doing what they were supposed to do. It was hard to accept I was wrong, but I quickly realized that my people could be trusted. They just needed the right amount of direction and coaching.

Giving the weekly team meetings a structure that focuses on what people are accomplishing instead of what they're doing is making a huge difference. And I think it really motivates people. At the end of our last meeting, it was thrilling when Joe said he couldn't believe what he has achieved. And Maya was never a strong performer, but she's come up with some really great ideas and solutions lately.

My boss sure has made this easy. She gives us monthly updates on company performance that I can share with my team. They love to know where the company is doing well and how they have contributed, and they appreciate learning where we're struggling so they can help turn things around.

One of the top concepts explored in engagement surveys is the discovery of how employees respond to this statement: *I understand my company's strategic direction and how what I do aligns with it.* As Susan realized, managers need to be clear about the big picture, and employees need to understand it. When we consider the human element in performance, it is not enough to know what to do. It is also important to know the how, why, how well, and how often for people to bring their best ideas and contributions.

At the outset, leaders must articulate company direction, strategy, and business goals. Keep the message simple and straightforward, and don't assume it's a once-a-year undertaking. In fact, touching on priority goals at least briefly in every team meeting helps employees continue to feel part of a common cause, especially if they are working from home. Remind people of your organization's purpose and ask them how they contribute to it. Even when they feel isolated, they need to know they make a difference. Most employees are concerned about overall company performance. You can put their minds at ease by sharing market realities with them and letting them know what is happening in other regions and business units, as well as with their customers. Be honest while maintaining a degree of optimism and a forward perspective. Share progress and accomplishments, no matter how small, and inform them how these accomplishments support organizational goals.

Throughout 2020 and into 2021, we saw many examples of our clients communicating honestly with employees as they helped them deal with the unknown while maintaining optimism. One client, a national property management company, was committed to retaining its workforce despite severe economic hardship. Employees were aware that the organization was doing everything in its power to avoid layoffs or furloughs despite significant losses in revenue and profitability. Leadership held steadfast to this commitment through the end of 2020, not wanting to eliminate jobs during the holiday season. They finally began the process of force reduction in late January 2021, but by that time, employees knew the company had done everything it could to avoid that action, and it was not unexpected.

Our own company, Ideal Outcomes, was faced with the same kind of challenges when clients understandably cut back their budgets. Jason, our CEO, provided updates at weekly online team calls regarding the status of client projects and proposals. Rather than furlough or lay people off, he honestly explained the situation to each employee individually and asked everyone to take a pay cut, making it clear he understood if they needed to reduce their hours. Everyone remained fully engaged with a commitment to quality and service that never faltered. We found ways to streamline our work and convert our content to online delivery, which was widely applauded and adopted by clients.

The bottom line is that you need to be authentic and communicate as a real person, not as a suit with a carefully constructed script. Avoid platitudes and clichés like "the customer comes first." Instead, share a story of an employee who exemplified great service. A real-life example resonates to much greater effect.

Goal Management Skills and Behaviors

Let's begin our look at goal management by looking back. Consider the productivity of each of your employees before the last crisis struck. If an individual was typically on task, meeting goals and deadlines, and collaborating with others, did this change when circumstances changed to remote work?

The wisest course a manager can take is to establish clear goals and accountabilities and create a regular process for check-ins so employees are not caught by surprise if projects aren't progressing. In reality, if we make expectations clear and follow up on them, we will be a lot less worried and a lot more trustful, regardless of where employees and managers are sitting. There is something extremely interesting about being trusted: Most people do not want to let down someone who trusts them and will work very hard to avoid doing so.

Accountability starts with clearly defined performance goals and a commitment to track those goals. Simply put, good goal management helps people focus on the right things. Numerous studies regarding the impact of goal management on productivity have supported the foundational research done in 1968 by Edwin Locke (University of Maryland) and Gary Latham (University of Toronto). They took a psychological approach and found that hard goals produce a higher level of performance than easy goals and that specific hard goals produce a higher level of output than a goal of "do your best."[26]

Ever wonder why effective goal setting continues to challenge organizations? After all, it seems to be common sense that if employees know what you want them to do, they will be much more likely to do it. Effective goal setting is complex and requires several well-executed strategies and adaptive management skills to be successful.

One way to determine whether you are doing a good job executing a strong performance management process is to consider how your employees might respond to these statements, which are commonly posed to employees in engagement surveys. These are fundamental to a successful performance management process.

1. I know exactly what I am expected to accomplish in my job.

2. My pay and career opportunities are impacted in part by how well I execute my goals.

3. My manager and I review and update my goals throughout the year to ensure they stay aligned with changes in company needs or strategy.

4. My manager gives me regular feedback on my performance.

5. My manager involves me in the goal setting process.

The fifth concept is important because it creates employee buy-in. As Dale Carnegie perfectly and succinctly stated many years ago, "People will support the world they create."

Your first step is to effectively communicate organizational purpose and goals. Along with that, you will need to develop goals for yourself (in partnership with your boss), and then share your own goals with employees. Ask them if they see and appreciate how your goals tie to company goals. Then ask them to articulate what they can do to support those goals and make them happen. Discuss this upfront with your team in a fun, stimulating, brainstorming session and you'll promote teamwork. Once team goals are delineated, each employee can develop their individual goals. Look for opportunities for employees to create both individual and shared goals.

Help your employees fine-tune their goals to make sure they are specific enough to be measurable, challenging enough to be motivating, and realistic enough not to be demotivating. Assist them with the wording by asking questions of them rather than simply telling them what to change. For example: How are you going to measure that? How long do you think this will take? Have you considered XYZ?

In this age of extreme change and disruption, managers must guide employees to the knowledge that they must not only own their goals but also expect and embrace the reality that goals will inevitably change. According to Ben Wingert and Heather Barrett of Gallup, "Employees and managers should be on the lookout for opportunities to pivot with changes to business needs and be rewarded for identifying new ways to make a positive impact. Managers should be given the expectation, authority and flexibility to tailor goal setting to the team and the individual as their work changes."[27]

When employees know what is expected and they have ownership in creating their own goals, they are much more likely to be committed, motivated, and focused. Link their goal to organizational purpose to help employees see that they make a difference, that their contributions matter. Make it clear that by meeting goals, the organization, employees, and customers all mutually benefit. In this way, you create an engaged passionate workforce and drive organizational success.

Follow Up Often

Accountability can be regarded as expecting that you might have to justify your actions to others in relation to a preexisting norm. In other words, the norm might be that team members are expected to complete projects and tasks on time and with quality, and as a team member, you will need to either comply with that norm or be able to justify why you have deviated from it. And there are consequences for meeting or deviating from preexisting norms.

In a *Fast Company* article, Kristen Berman, a founding member of the behavioral economics group at Google, cited two interesting examples of the power of making accountability public:[28]

1. In Ely, Iowa, voting rates were driven 6.9 percent higher when voters were told that if they didn't vote, their names would be published in the newspaper.

2. A YMCA's attendance increased by 17 percent to 23 percent after informing its members how often their peers went to the gym and that their attendance would be publicized the following month.

We do not suggest that employees who miss goals or deadlines be subject to public exposure. Far from it. Apart from being demotivating, such an action is certainly not acceptable leadership behavior. But that research does demonstrate the power of accountability, and there are ways that managers can use group accountability in productive and motivating ways.

Team meetings are an obvious opportunity to review team progress. Weekly meetings that last no more than an hour keep the team focused and reduce isolation. Less frequent meetings are not productive because they tend to run longer. Establish a routine and use a platform for these meetings that allows you to share documents and enable face time for all participants. You might want to encourage everyone to stay on camera throughout the meeting if they can to help minimize distractions, reduce the likelihood of multitasking, and provide visual connection. Make these calls two-way by having each team member summarize what they are working on.

Make these events positive. You want people to look forward to them. Give them the opportunity to ask for and offer assistance. Build trust by sharing not only what you personally have accomplished but also what may not have been successful. Announce your plans for the following week, including what you will do differently to achieve positive outcomes, and have employees do the same.

Concentrate on accomplishments. Questions such as "What are you working on?" encourage open discussion. Also be sure to ask, "Where do you need help?" and foster collaboration by encouraging team members to provide assistance to those who need it. Recognize that you do not have to have all the solutions. Adaptive leaders empower their teams to solve problems and offer solutions.

Be sure to end on a positive note. For example, go around the room, whether virtually or face to face, asking everyone to share one thing of which they are particularly proud from the previous week. You want them to walk away feeling engaged, inspired, and confident. Be generous with your praise and thank everyone for being a great team player.

In addition to team meetings, managers should meet one-on-one with individuals consistently and regularly. The desirable frequency varies depending on several factors. Less experienced employees, individuals who are struggling with remote work, and those handling mission-critical projects or tight deadlines require more frequent touchpoints. When you are working remotely, you will not bump into employees in the hall or be able to casually poke your head into their office. Because of that, you will need to intentionally create some of those moments, so in addition to set meetings, pick up the phone a few times a month to informally check in.

Considering that managers not only supervise the work of others but also have their own work and a boss to whom they are account-able, it is important to manage these meetings so they don't impact the manager's own productivity. But this is not the time to be hands-off. Without regular touchpoints, you leave a lot to chance and miss opportunities to build and sustain relationships with your employees.

You can minimize the impact on your own productivity by scheduling one-on-ones in blocks of time—for example, every Thursday morning from nine to noon. If you do this regularly, most sessions should be short. That means thirty minutes at most. Meet with an employee twice a month and you will be able to touch base with six direct reports a month. If your team is larger, add a second time slot.

Another way to reduce the impact of these sessions on your time is to make employees own the process. Tell them to come prepared to report on goal status, barriers they have encountered, and successes. Use these meetings to tweak goals when business needs have changed, to recognize and celebrate success, and to course correct when necessary.

Take advantage of technology as well. There are many collaborative tools with which employees can post their accomplishments in advance of the call, thereby saving your time and increasing their accountability. You could make such postings visible to the entire team so everyone can see what others are working on, which has the additional benefit of creating the public accountability discussed earlier. Provide ongoing feedback and remember that it can be given in many forms. One-on-one conversation is essential, but feedback can also be as simple as a text or an email.

Although it is important to structure touchpoints, it is not possible or even reasonable to create all those that naturally occur in an office setting. The challenge is to find the right balance to stay connected, collaborating and motivating without making employees feel you are micromanaging or demonstrating a lack of trust.

Bottom line: Ditch your trust issues and learn more about employees' workstyles and talents before rushing to judge their performance. Use this knowledge to leverage the different talents of your team to get the job done and improve employee job satisfaction.

Implement OKR Methodology

Feedback is a time-proven strategy to engage employees. A study by Gallup in 2019 found that feedback dramatically increases remote worker engagement.[29]

OKR goal setting is a structured methodology for giving timely feedback that makes managers' lives easier while inspiring higher engagement and performance from employees. First introduced by Andy Grove at Intel in the 1970s, it contains three critical components: objectives, key results, and follow-up.

Objectives

Objectives are big picture and qualitative in nature and should be inspirational and exciting. Think of them as a mini-mission for a specific period of time—typically a quarter, although shorter time frames, such as a month, can be appropriate. Objectives give organizations, teams, and/or individuals a rallying cry. In a bold manner, they tell us where we want to go, and they get us all rowing in the same direction. An example of such an objective might be as follows: Create an organizational culture that makes us an employer of choice.

To achieve this objective, senior leaders must set the stage by establishing organizational objectives. Business units and teams can then establish their own objectives to support the organization-wide objectives, preferably with input from all employees.

Key Results

Key results (KRs) are focused and quantitative. They tell us how well we are progressing toward our objectives. A rule of thumb is to establish about three results for each objective since it is impossible to handle greater numbers without watering them all down. KRs quickly tell us if we are on the right track or need to shift focus. Organizations typically use KRs such as growth, employee engagement, market share, and quality, but they can measure other results, depending on the objective such as Net Promoter Scores or other measurements of customer satisfaction, employee turnover, quality of hire, or customer retention.

The key to effective KRs is twofold: First, they should be developed by the team or individual accountable for achieving them. Remember, people own the world they create, and we want people to own these results. Second, they should be challenging but achievable. If they're too hard, people give up. If they're too easy, you're not doing anything to inspire exceptional performance. You want to push people and stretch them so their sense of pride is palpable when the KR is achieved.

Follow-Up

Follow-up, along with regular communication, is critical. How often? As with other things, timing partly depends on the level of employee experience. Green employees might need follow-up almost daily as they ramp up their learning curve, while seasoned employees will not require much hand-holding. Many of our clients apply an agile approach. They hold short weekly meetings at which everyone working toward the objective and the KRs briefly share progress, ask for help where needed, and discuss potential barriers to success. They also share next steps—what they are going to accomplish in the following week. It is useful to take a team pulse. How confident are they overall that the KRs will be met? Such meetings can be held in small groups or with individual employees, depending on the nature of the project.

Follow-up also includes celebrating successes. A weekly or biweekly meeting solely centered on sharing successes, giving people bragging rights, and spotlighting achieved KRs or progress keeps engagement high and builds teamwork. Imagine the impact when the sales team thanks the service team for helping them retain a major customer or reports on the delivery of three new contracts. And for the remote employee, catering lunch to their home is a nice treat. Develop your own traditions, such as a rotating trophy or other symbol of success, and invite senior executives to attend.

Managers who set inspiring objectives, track and measure them with targeted, challenging key results, and follow up on progress are well on their way to creating and sustaining a high-performance culture.

Use Online Tools to Add Spark to Meetings

Many online tools can be used to add spark to both business *meetings* and business *social interactions*.

Slack is a popular real-time chat tool that also reduces email. Teleconferencing is important. For groups and one-on-one meetings, Zoom is free and easy to use. A paid subscription gives you access to breakout rooms where employees can get into smaller groups to brainstorm and problem solve and then come back to the group as a whole to present their ideas. Google Hangouts allows up to twenty-five participants. GoToMeeting and WebEx are also great for team meetings. If you want a quick way to share screens one-on-one, try join.me or Microsoft Teams.

Look into an array of online tools aimed at bringing spark to remote meetings. Gathertown, for example, allows you to create rooms with themes. Although primarily for conferences, the platform allows for networking sessions where groups can gather. Other examples include Kumospace and Pluto, both of which incorporate spatial dynamics that allow users to move around and interact on virtual maps. They work well for socializing and recreating happy hour.

Enabling employees to work remotely is going to continue to be a management responsibility. When managers fail to communicate (whether in an office or in a remote setting), engagement plummets. When managers step up and have frequent, meaningful conversations, employees thrive.

Ideas for Managing Remotely

Here are some real-world examples that illustrate ways in which you can effectively manage on a remote basis.

Focus on Values: The VP of Human Resources at a large retailer wanted to build energy and camaraderie across her geographically diverse team located at the corporate headquarters and three regional offices. In addition, she wanted to inspire risk-taking, a company value with which many employees struggled. Her idea was the "giraffe award"—because giraffes stick their necks out.

Each month, the entire group of fifty employees met. Some were physically in the same room and others attended via videoconferencing. One week before the meeting, everyone was asked to vote on the next recipient of the giraffe award, a charming, plush, two-foot model. The giraffe was handed in person to the winner if they were located at the corporate office or shipped to the employee if they were regionally based. That giraffe was proudly displayed on the winner's desk all month until it was presented to the next recipient the following month.

Make It Fun and Memorable

It was the holiday season, and the customer service manager was feeling the impact of workers spread out around the city. He was longing for the days when everyone could get together in a break room and have a holiday potluck and some kind of silly gift exchange, and he decided to handle it remotely using Microsoft Teams.

Ahead of the team lunch, participants sent recipes to each other for what they planned to cook and eat. They also were emailed the name of the person for whom they were to buy a small gift, which they shipped to the colleague with strict instructions to leave the gift unopened in advance of the potluck. At the event, everyone displayed their meal on camera, ate, talked, and had a wonderful time. Then each employee opened their gift.

The employees enjoyed the time so much, the team decided to hold the luncheon once a quarter (minus the gifts). Most of them happily reported how much their families enjoyed the leftovers!

Create Connection

One of our clients dedicates a few minutes at the beginning of each meeting to open-ended, non-work-related questions such as "What are your weekend plans?" or "What did you do last weekend?" If someone recently took time off, he asks about the vacation. This gives employees time to connect personally with each other as they probably would if they were in an office setting walking down the hall. He also makes sure to regularly create personal time with employees by inviting one or two at a time to join him for a virtual lunch. Conversation during these lunches flows naturally from personal to work just as it would face-to-face in a restaurant or the company breakroom.

Increase Recognition

A sales manager knew her team was struggling with remote client sales calls. She created an online page using Slack where sales reps could post their own success stories, as well as the success stories of colleagues. The page took on a force of its own very quickly. Several reps posted comments from clients and many shared ideas on how to overcome barriers to closing deals. When leaders support their employees' self-sufficiency, they inspire confidence in achieving their own goals and open their willingness to take risks, learn, and grow.

Performance management is much more than filling out a performance review form once a year. Adaptive leaders ignite their organizational culture by building the relationships and connections with employees that inspire and sustain exceptional performance.

5

Build Capability and Develop Your Talent

"The world is moving so fast that we have few true experts on tomorrow. All we have are experts on yesterday."
—Gyan Nagpal, author, *The Future Ready Organization*

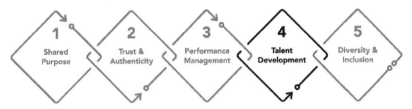

Eleven Months

I am really proud of my team. Several of them took the lead when it came to using online tools to deliver training to each other. Maria realized that customer delivery teams around the country were duplicating efforts. We were chatting in our weekly team meeting about some of the issues we were having, and she piped up, "Do you think other teams have this problem? Why don't we ever talk with them?"

I guess we were each so focused on our little worlds that we didn't think about other teams. But once we all started working from home, the concept of "our team" or "our office" shifted. Maria called a few reps in other cities, and it turned out that some of them had the same issues. Fortunately, the team in Seattle had figured out a great solution.

Next thing I knew, Maria had set up a training for the whole country. The Seattle folks delivered their approach online, and it was spot on. She did a great job lending her expertise with online training and helped the Seattle group make the experience interactive and fun. As a result of that experience, two members of each of our five regional customer delivery teams now meet once a month and take best practices back to their local groups.

I honestly don't think we would have done this had we not been forced out of the office. Our world had to get smaller for us to think about how to make it larger.

One of the first casualties of a financial crisis is often the company's training budget. While it may be a quick way to effect cost savings, it is not the right solution. We don't say this simply because we passionately believe ongoing talent development is critical and have a vested interest in providing it to companies large and small. We say it because the data is clear that cutting a training budget is a short-term fix at best with many long-term downsides.

McKinsey cites a Training Industry Report, which showed that during and after the Great Recession, a significant drop in training expenditures in the years 2009 and 2010 was followed by a surge in 2011 and a return to 2008 levels in 2012. Says McKinsey, "What this tells us is that if companies cut their learning budgets now, they're only delaying their investment, not netting a saving—especially since the current crisis will require a larger skill shift than the 2008 financial crisis did."[30]

McKinsey further states, "Leaders should pursue a broad reskilling agenda that develops employees' digital experience and their cognitive, emotional, and adaptability skills. Companies can't be resilient if their workforces aren't. Building your reskilling muscle now is the first step to ensuring that your organization's recovery business model is a success."

There are a number of similarities between the 2008 financial crisis and the 2020 pandemic. In both cases, they occurred very quickly, truly blindsiding the country. Very few businesses or government leaders saw either crisis coming their way. Both events created a significant fear of the unknown as well as potential long-term impact. Some organizations are still recovering from the market crash. The pandemic created uncertainty as well. We are still not sure how certain industries will recover and how many aspects of life will face a permanent so-called "new normal."

There is nothing like a crisis to spotlight your capability gaps. At the same time, it is apparent that companies with adaptive leaders and strong capabilities are positioned to overcome challenges and focus on what is relevant.

Technology is a key enabler of that focus. It is a tool that allows for a more hybrid, fluid workforce, but it is no more than that. It is simply a tool. Top ManpowerGroup executives Becky Frankiewicz and Tomas Chamorro-Premuzic, wrote in the *Harvard Business Review*, "Culture doesn't exist within walls; it exists within people, so you have to build culture through people, wherever they sit."[31] An essential component of building and sustaining your culture is creating talent within your organization, not just recruiting it externally.

Developing Talent Within

In its thought-provoking paper, "The Social Enterprise and Work: Paradox as a Path Forward," Deloitte homed in on several leading human capital trends. At its core is the concept that business needs to see itself as a social enterprise "whose mission combines revenue growth and profit-making with the need to respect and support its environment and stakeholder network."[32]

When we think about respecting and supporting the stakeholder network—and in particular, supporting our employees—it becomes clear that we also need to think differently about training and development. The future, as we have learned rather painfully, is uncertain. And it will continue to be so. Timely, effective response becomes nearly impossible with the rapid speed of change we now see in the world.

Many leaders concentrate on "reskilling" their workforce. The challenge with reskilling is that needed skills are a rapidly shifting target. There are skills gaps, and they are almost impossible to define. The pace of change is so fast that it outpaces efforts to reskill. You're always playing catch-up. The focus instead should be on giving people the knowhow to reinvent themselves by providing development on the competencies needed to be more adaptive and flexible. Challenge your employees to identify their strengths and where they need to grow.

The qualities that workers and companies need for tomorrow are not what they were yesterday. Jobs have changed, and the way we conduct business has changed. Precisely calibrated skills can become a barrier to innovative thinking and flexibility. Skills are still important, but today's success also requires innovation and entrepreneurship, adaptability, collaboration, and emotional intelligence.

Middle managers hold the key to creating tomorrow's team today. Because they sit between leadership and front-line employees, they have a solid perspective on cultural reality—what the workplace is truly like. It also enables them to be the voice for a range of information going out to the organization, including the messages leadership needs to hear from individual contributors. Middle managers are uniquely positioned to take the helm in demonstrating a willingness to embrace new technology, remain calm under pressure, and embrace empathetic leadership. Above all, they serve as role models to their employees when they are willing to learn, take risks, and champion diverse ideas. As Microsoft CEO Satya Nadella says, "The learn-it-all does better than the know-it-all."

A main driver of middle management success is empowerment. An over-used word? Perhaps. But without it, middle managers are powerless to drive change and influence the culture in a positive way.

Without the trust of leadership (and trust is the lynchpin of empowerment), managers know they are ineffectual, which impacts their confidence, and employees know it, which impacts their motivation to engage. Managers need to be able to take risks and even make mistakes with some level of impunity. That is how people learn. Of course, this does not mean leaders should take a completely hands-off approach, but if they are clear about expectations and what managers will be held accountable for, they can give managers greater decision-making latitude. Leaders who coach, who ask questions rather than tell managers what to do, serve as role models for how middle managers should treat their direct reports.

Who "Owns" Employee Development?

It looks like a paradigm shift is under way. In the past, many organizations put more of the accountability for workforce development on the individual employee, but according to a Deloitte survey, 73 percent of workers believe organizations hold the primary responsibility for it. Amazon is a prime example (pun intended) of a company that has taken the lead. In 2019, it committed to investing over $700 million to upskill one hundred thousand employees across the US.[33] Most of this investment focuses on technological skills, from essentials to cloud computing, robotics, and machine learning.

We do not question the need for organizations to upskill employees in technology, but this alone is not sufficient. Organizations must address the need to expand workers' abilities at all levels to dynamically deal with change and embrace continuous learning and adaptation. They must also learn how to better leverage networks of teams who may be sitting anywhere on the globe. Another way of thinking about this is to consider how we can better anticipate what workers will need to know to build their capacity to solve as yet unforeseen problems while *simultaneously* addressing current skill gaps. As part of this strategy, organizations need to find ways to retool the millions of workers whose jobs were permanently lost due to the pandemic.

There are three areas in which companies can develop a new employee development strategy: shifting toward an emphasis on broad capability rather than specific skills, leveraging employee talents based on interests and strengths, and creating a truly blended approach between formal and on-the-job development of soft skills.

Building Broad Capability

Building broad capability is challenging because capabilities comprise not only the technical skills and knowledge people have, but also their attributes, attitudes, and behaviors. What is required is a mind shift from "training du jour" and reactive curricula to a comprehensive, strategic approach to learning and development. And leaders must accept that performance cannot always receive more emphasis than learning and experience.

What do we mean by that? Think about your typical customer service performance environment. Each week, the manager goes over the number of calls, talk time, problem resolution stats, and other performance criteria. But what if the manager was committed to the team's capability development? She will still focus on the service performance data, but she might also ask questions that focus on learning and experience: What did you learn this week about our customer experience? Which solutions elicited the most positive response from customers? Did you try anything different to solve that problem?

Leveraging Employee Talents Based on Interests and Strengths

The evidence for concentrating on employees' strengths is overwhelming. Gallup has studied this concept extensively and found that when supervisors adopted this approach, there was only a one in a hundred chance of employees becoming disengaged. And nearly two thirds of employees whose strengths were recognized were actively engaged, which was twice the nationwide average.[34]

Assessing employees' strengths is not difficult. We find a combination works best: formal assessment such as Gallup's Strength Finders or the Personal Strengths Profile along with conversations between the employee and their manager. In addition to strengths/personality assessments, leaders can take advantage of 360 assessments, which can be powerful tools when used in conjunction with coaching and other development. (Note that we do not recommend 360 assessments for performance management purposes, but only for development.) Analyze assignments and projects to determine what skills and competencies are required for success, then map employee strengths to these. Be sure to build diverse teams where strengths are balanced. Pair up-and-coming individuals with a mentor.

A Truly Blended Approach

Activities to enable people to acquire new capabilities should include on-the-job training, developmental job assignments, conferences, cohort groups, job shadowing, coaching, and mentoring, as well as formal classroom training.

Many organizations waste valuable investments in formal training by not aligning it with coaching, mentoring, special projects, and work assignments. Middle managers, in particular, need to be invested in this process. There is great value in following up with employees, discussing what was learned, and collaborating with them to find ways to apply learning on the job. Managers can also coach employees on applying what they learned and talk about how such application enhances productivity and/or other important job performance measurements. This increases motivation and engagement along with reinforcing learning and enhancing performance.

Cohort groups are meaningful ways to reinforce and sustain formal learning. We work with clients to establish cohorts of employees who will attend formal trainings together over time. This builds camaraderie and creates a natural support group with which employees can share successes, work through challenges together, or simply ask for help. We couple such programs with a variety of sustainability strategies.

For example, one client, a large public utility company, has partnered with us to develop their director level leaders. The same twenty directors attend a series of training programs based on their seven leadership competencies. They also attend sustainability sessions four to six weeks following the formal training during which they report on progress and share successes. Although not formally part of this program, the cohorts, all from different divisions of the organization, frequently develop informal networks and support each other regularly with their business process improvement plans as they enhance their leadership skills.

Another client, a national member services organization, has built their learning and development strategy around a cohort model. Whether the formal training is focused on sales, leadership, customer service, or other operational teams, cohorts create a strong and lasting level of internal networking and support. Shared experiences instill a sense of belonging and build trust across cross-functional groups. The cohorts rely on each other when there are challenges, and they celebrate successes together. Relationships built during their development experiences create lasting networks, even after people get promoted or relocate to other parts of the company. Such relationships create strong motivation to continue applying what was learned in the program.

Human Capital Versus Social Capital

University professor and respected thought leader Dave Ulrich has conducted research showing that building organizational capabilities to improve innovation, enhance collaboration, reduce bureaucratic barriers, and open participation delivers returns *four times greater* than developing individual talent. In his book *Victory Through Organization*,

Ulrich explains that the entire workforce flourishes when you improve the workplace.

David Forman, author of *Fearless HR* and former CLO of the Human Capital Institute, agrees. "Talent is more important than ever as we strive to address unpredictable events and futures, but we must use a more complete lens. It is less about individuals and more about cross-functional and self-governing teams. It is less about trying to manage and control talented individuals than unleashing the potential of all colleagues. Increasingly, what you know (human capital) is dependent on who you know and collaborate with (social capital)."[35]

An emphasis on collaboration is essential for organizations to build employee and company resilience in a constantly changing world. Collaboration is the foundation for knowledge transfer and the ability to flex employee skills, deploying them where they are needed and most effective. In fact, 75 percent of organizations surveyed by Deloitte stated that "creating and preserving knowledge across evolving workforces is important or very important for their success." In contrast, only nine percent were ready to address this trend.[36]

Part of the challenge to effectively manage knowledge is that it is often treated as something that happens separately from the work performed. Leaders must recognize that knowledge management is not simply documenting and disseminating knowledge. It is, more importantly, *applying* knowledge to actions and decision-making and using knowledge to drive innovation. Until you can derive value from the knowledge and data you collect, it will not add value to your organization or to your customers.

Many organizations are probably correct in their belief that they lack the right technology, including data analytics and AI, to create effective digital knowledge sharing. But as noted earlier, technology is a tool. Your culture must enable and support teamwork and collaboration or the best tools will buy you little gain. The number one people barrier to sharing and using knowledge is the existence of organizational silos, not the lack of technology.

Early on, Sodexo, a global food services and facilities management company, recognized the value of collaboration, knowledge sharing, and diversity. Their Spirit of Mentoring program connects employees to engage with one another as learners and advisors, to transfer knowledge, and to collaborate on learning, career development, and on-the-job productivity.[37]

Google's Googler-to-Googler program provides as much as 80 percent of their tracked learning offerings. In this approach, over six thousand Google employees have become volunteer trainers, sharing their expertise with others. It is a program that clearly recognizes the right and need for employees to learn. It also acknowledges that a great deal of learning can come from other employees who have valuable experience worth sharing.[38]

Leaders should consider deploying strategies like these in their own organizations:

- Leverage technology so employees can readily connect with each other regardless of their role or where they are located.

- Don't reinvent the wheel. Tap into existing employee groups such as culture committees or employee resource groups such as diversity or professional development groups.

- Model the way for collaboration by eliminating silos at the top and establishing cultural expectations for teamwork and knowledge sharing.

- Recognize that an important purpose of gathering and sharing knowledge is to create new and innovative solutions to problems.

- Create learning cohorts as described earlier to reinforce application and ensure consistency.

Focus More than Ever on Soft Skills

People need training on technology and on the specific skills required to do their jobs, but it is competencies such as communication, empathy, collaboration, and problem-solving that will move organizations in the right direction for years to come. Prioritize these skills and make the commitment to drive them deep into your company.

Every year, LinkedIn analyzes its huge professional social network and publishes a "Top Skills" list ranking the skills that are in top demand but low in supply. The 2019 and 2020 reports from LinkedIn place soft skills at the top, and in 2020, the top five skills listed by them were creativity, persuasion, collaboration, adaptability, and emotional intelligence.[39] You might wish to expand this list, adding navigating and leading in a network of teams and solving problems from the customer's perspective.

In a study that correlated soft skills with performance, Global HR consulting firm DDI found that empathy was the number one interaction skill driving overall performance, decision-making, coaching, engaging, planning, and organizing. Unfortunately, empathy was one of the lowest scoring skills among the frontline leaders they assessed.[40]

The Society for Human Resources (SHRM) took a slightly different approach by looking at the top skills missing in job applicants. In short supply were problem-solving, the ability to deal with complexity and ambiguity, and communication.

One of the reasons organizations hesitate to invest in soft skills development is that these programs have not demonstrated much impact, primarily because organizations do not define upfront why they are targeting such development and the goals they want to achieve. Even if they define the purpose, they do not align it with business objectives. You can develop a more successful soft skills strategy with the following approaches.

Determine the Right Development Team

Human Resources cannot tackle this project alone. Put together a team of ten to twelve people who have strong soft skills and represent various operational functions: field employees, frontline employees, and middle managers, along with a couple of leaders who will champion the cause. Include one or two high potential employees who, if they have been identified wisely, will possess many of the skills you want to develop in others.

Begin with a Focus on Business Needs

What's going on in your business? What are your top two or three business strategies? What aspects of your business have priority? For example, do you want to improve employee engagement and talent retention? Do you need to increase revenues from existing customers? When you begin with focusing on business needs, you avoid falling into the trap of implementing "programs du jour." More importantly, you lay the foundation for measuring the impact of your initiatives on business performance. For example, if increasing innovation is a business need, you can determine the value of your programs by looking at increased patents applied for, increased revenues from new products, numbers of expanded product lines, or other measures of importance.

Consider Your Culture

Consider your culture, including your purpose and values. How will your development programs support, align with, and reinforce your corporate culture in a consistent manner? For example, if teamwork is a core value, reinforce this value by creating cohorts of participants who coach each other on implementing the concepts taught in their training.

Determine What Is Important

Determine the soft skills most impactful for achieving your business strategies while aligning with your culture and values. For example, if customer satisfaction scores are low, look at the skill sets demonstrated by your customer interaction personnel. Are they friendly? Are they good listeners? How well do they manage their time and follow-up? What are the typical service complaints? Are they product related or people related?

If a goal is to increase innovation, what behaviors are lacking that drive innovation? Are talented employees micromanaged, for example? Are managers good at supporting risk-taking or are mistakes harshly criticized? This is a simple yet compelling and relevant way to perform a business-focused needs analysis and tie your interventions to business impact. When most employees are working from home, the importance of these skills is amplified. Communication skills are more vital than ever during online conferencing, in email, and in chat tools.

Consider the Importance of Empathy

As discussed earlier, empathy is essential, but it is in short supply. There are many definitions of empathy, perhaps the simplest being the ability to sense and be sensitive to others' feelings coupled with the ability to imagine what they might be feeling or thinking. Empathy is tied to emotional intelligence, and many researchers have proven empathy to be a requirement for successful leadership. No matter what your other business needs are, you can safely assume this gap exists in your organization, especially if remote work is in the mix. The challenge is to determine where these empathy gaps lie and what the associated behavioral gaps are.

Consider Using Assessment Tools

Assessment tools that can help include the MBTI (Myers Briggs), which is useful for determining personality styles and whether you have a balanced workforce, and the Personal Strengths Profile (PSP), which gives insight into personality, communication, and problem-solving styles. Harvard's Professional Development Extension School recommends these tools: MindTools Quizzes and these resources: Institute for Health and Human Potential, and TalentSmart.

Tools like these can help you analyze gaps more specifically so you can develop programs to address them. 360 assessments can offer insight into your management and leadership soft skills, as do data from employee and engagement surveys. Look for patterns of gaps and concentrate on your most important issues. We coach clients on how to use these tools effectively because there are pitfalls when 360 tools are poorly executed, but when they are done well, the value of the information gained is significant.

Plan Your Curriculum and Delivery Methods

Once you have a solid understanding of your business needs, the soft skills required to drive them, and the gaps in your organization, you are ready to design your program strategy. Take into consideration that such skills require practice and feedback. With many employees working remotely, self-paced online programs or live online coaching are necessary and effective approaches (when done right). Consider cohort development as well, where you create groups of peers who coach and give ongoing feedback to each other following meetings, team discussions, or agile scrum sessions. With the right technology, these all can be handled online.

Measure Progress and Results

Develop a simple, visual scorecard to track your progress quarterly. Data points to include are relevant business metrics including customer satisfaction scores, feedback from program participants, shifts in 360 scores, data from spot employee surveys, and turnover.

Base your tracking on the goals you established at the beginning of the process. Report on results regularly to your leaders.

Customize

Off-the-shelf programs rarely resonate with participants. Learners need to see the connection between content, your culture, your business, and your work environment. If your organization does not have learning and development capacity in-house, partner with a vendor who is adept at content and delivery customization.

Good vendors will invest time in getting to know your work environment and culture and will incorporate your language into the content. They will make sure your goals and priorities are emphasized, and the people delivering the programs will speak your company's language. One thing we have learned is that people tend to be literal and quickly dismiss training content that does not align with the work world they know. Simple things such as how you refer to employees (team members, associates) or customers (clients) impact delivery credibility with your participants.

Long-term job and organizational success depend heavily on soft skills mastery. That can be accomplished online, but it takes time. So the sooner you start, the sooner there will be a positive impact on your organization.

Continue to Enhance Your Digital Learning Capabilities

Digital solutions are here to stay. Companies have realized that online training not only gets results (if done well) but is also cost effective. Even before the pandemic, our Ideal Outcomes team had begun to transition content into an online format—in part based on our recognition of the need and in part because of requests from clients.

With the onset of COVID-19, some clients—national and international firms with employees running into the tens of thousands—

reacted quickly, wishing to convert classes that were already on their calendar. We responded with agility and flexibility, adapting a wide range of programs including intensive four- or five-day "train the trainer" programs and eight-week, three-and-a-half-hour sessions for upper-level managers. We also converted top-level leadership development courses and programs for mid-level managers to online offerings. Popular topics included communication skills, leadership, customer service, sales, and time management.

Our goal, first and foremost, was to replicate the interactive, behavioral, and performance-based experience of face-to-face classes in an online format. Knowledge retention was a priority, which meant making the online programs interactive from the moment an individual logged on. It meant having participants engage each other in breakout rooms, write on a white board, enter comments in a chat room, respond to polling questions, virtually raise their hands, and listen to the input of their colleagues. We made sure participants were actively involved in their learning from the beginning to the end of a session.

Another important aspect of our methodology was to create a learning environment that would motivate and enable participant change. To achieve change, we believe an emotional shift is equal to behavior change in importance. Without emotional change, people will do something differently if they are required to, but they will often slip back into past habits unless they have a fundamental shift in thinking, attitude, commitment, and/or other emotional factors.

Trainers also need to understand that real growth and change not only takes time but also requires effective feedback, which means incorporating rigorous coaching into program delivery. A safe and trusting environment is essential to "coach in the moment." That means trainers must model coaching techniques, including asking for permission to give feedback and maintaining a high level of engagement from all participants.

A few logistics need to be taken under consideration when you plan online training. From our perspective, most online classes require the commitment of two people: a virtual instructor with specialized facilitation skills and a certified digital producer. The producer facilitates the technology and troubleshoots any problems participants encounter so the trainer can remain focused on the participants. The instructor and producer need to work together seamlessly to make sure everything runs smoothly.

Developing content specifically for online delivery is also essential. We quickly learned that you can't deliver as much information in the same time frame as you can in person. That's because time is taken up with the technology: moving people in and out of breakout rooms and the time they take thinking about their responses before typing them in the chat or on a virtual white board. Even with producers working their magic in the background, technical challenges occur and delays happen.

You might encounter some reluctance and hesitancy from potential participants, especially with regard to multi-day programs. Many people have experienced deadly webinars and one-way training, making them skeptical that they could stay attentive and enthusiastic during an eight-hour online day. These objections can be quickly overcome when trainees experience the tools of an interactive training scenario in the right hands.

The learning landscape has changed in ways that will foster a new way of thinking about learning, development, and collaboration. The adoption of fully digitized approaches to recreate the best of in-person learning through live video and social sharing is an essential enterprise strategy. This transformation makes it possible to scale learning efforts in a more cost-effective way and permits greater personalization for learners—and, in turn, greater effectiveness.

Companies around the world have had to vault ahead in adopting and applying digital technology. The future will be owned by those organizations that can be nimbler and more adaptable to any crisis.

People development is paramount to igniting your culture. When you continuously invest in your people, you create and sustain the energy, drive, and ability to thrive in an ever-increasing competitive and challenging world. You reinforce shared beliefs, demonstrate core values, and unleash the talent needed to succeed.

6

Create Belonging through Diversity and Inclusion

"Diversity is the mix. Inclusion is making the mix work."
—Andres Tapia, Senior Client Partner, Korn Ferry

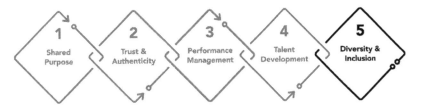

1	2	3	4	5
Shared Purpose	Trust & Authenticity	Performance Management	Talent Development	Diversity & Inclusion

Twelve Months

It's odd. In some ways, working from home has created unexpected opportunities for people around the country to work together. You would think being in the office would allow for that, but I suppose when you are on your own at home, you are more likely to reach out to others in your position in different regions for ideas and advice. There aren't many female managers in my region, and it has been very helpful to meet women in management who work in other regions. I never thought much about the lack of women in my own office before. It is something I have become accustomed to. It has been gratifying to meet my peers—and particularly my female peers.

It's not that I have been treated differently because I'm a woman. Our culture is not a good old boys club. But having a sense of belonging with other women managers has been a positive experience, and it is one I don't think I would have had if we hadn't start working remotely.

The cohesiveness we have created has improved so many of our processes. It also has increased the visibility of my team. My team is diverse, in part I think because as a woman of color, I have consciously tried to create that. I think sometimes they have felt . . . well, not excluded exactly, but that career advancement was going to be challenging. They do not see a lot of female leaders or people of color in leadership, at least in our region. We have been talking about starting some virtual diversity groups so we can connect with and even create different peer groups, and I am confident they will help build the confidence we all need to advance. I'm excited to be doing this across the country—no borders, so to speak. It will open doors for everyone.

Striving for diversity is not simply a politically correct, feel-good goal for corporations. While it is certainly an ethical imperative, organizations have increasingly recognized it is also good business. There is mounting research to prove the point from companies such as McKinsey & Company, Development Dimensions International (DDI), Korn Ferry, and Boston Consulting Group.

- A McKinsey study of 180 global publicly traded companies found that those whose executive boards had the most diversity showed returns on equity (ROE) 53 percent higher than those that were the least diverse.[41]

- A DDI survey of more than two thousand human resource executives and nearly sixteen thousand global leaders found that organizations with above-average diversity were eight times more likely to be in the top 10 percent for financial performance.[42]

- A Korn Ferry report found that companies in the top quartile of performance were 3.6 times more likely to include diversity and inclusion among their publicly professed values.[43]

- A Boston Consulting Group study discovered that innovation was the biggest benefit of enhanced diversity with earnings before interest and taxes (EBIT) margins 9 percent higher than their worst-performing competitors.[44]

- According to research by onboarding resource firm Sapling, while 64 percent of jobseekers actively seek a company that espouses diversity and inclusion, only 55 percent of people feel their company actively demonstrates diversity and inclusion.[45]

All this research leads to the conclusion neatly summarized by Laurence D. Fink, CEO and Founder of BlackRock, the world's largest investment firm handling nearly nine trillion dollars of investments. "If we are not a mirror of who are clients are, we're going to fail."

Many companies have talked a good game, promoting the virtues of diversity and inclusion, and not delivering, but increasingly, major organizations are making serious public commitments to enact real change. Early in 2021, the Silicon Valley Leadership Group (SVLG) unveiled its 25x25 initiative in which twenty companies including Facebook, Twitter, United Airlines, Alaska Airlines and the San Francisco 49ers pledged that by 2025, at least 25 percent of their leadership will be people of color and women.

The commitment is solid, said Ahmad Thomas, CEO of SVLG. "This isn't window dressing. It's not a feel-good letter that everyone can sign onto, then go back out on the golf course. There's a reason why we haven't seen anything like this: It's a feat."

Around the same time, McDonald's upped the ante by stating it will raise minority representation among senior executives from 29 percent to 35 percent within four years, and by 2030, it will have an equal number of men and women holding leadership positions. McDonald's learned the hard way. In 2020, it faced accusations of racism and was hit with lawsuits from Black executives and from current and former Black franchisees.[46] Late 2020, it hired a diversity officer to lead its diversity strategy.

Diversity at the top drives value and is critical at all levels of an organization to drive innovation and a sense of inclusion. It opens doors, facilitates communication, and broadens both perspective and thought. Diversity is complicated because its definition is . . . well . . . diverse. It encompasses all the differences that make us unique—not only race, color, ethnicity, and gender but also language, nationality, sexual orientation, religion, socioeconomic status, age, physical ability, and mental ability. And we cannot stop there. Also consider diversity of thought, of family status, of cultural background, and of political beliefs.

Rather than trying to figure out what diversity means, let's think about it from a different perspective: acceptance and respect. It means understanding that each individual is unique and being willing to recognize and value individual differences. When we consider the concepts of acceptance and respect, we shift our mindset. Diversity isn't simply having representation across multiple aspects of humanity. Rather, it is about how we react to those differences, and even how we feel about them.

Among other things, diversity is an intellectual concept. For that matter, so is inclusion, which is how well all these different types of people work together, are accepted, and feel about being in our workplace. The deeper question is whether we create a work environment where everyone feels fully accepted. This moves us toward the concept of belonging, which is not an intellectual concept at all. As Claudia Brind-Woody, vice president and managing director of intellectual property, IBM, says, "Inclusivity means not just 'we're allowed to be there,' but we are valued. I've always said: smart teams will do amazing things, but truly diverse teams will do impossible things." In other words, a sense of belonging leads to behavior that can make a positive difference within an organization.

Belonging doesn't just mean being accepted. It also means being fully involved and invested in the organization's purpose and its mission. Belonging fosters participation, buy-in, engagement, and trust. It also means being invited to participate and being made to feel welcome and valued. While it's always great to be invited to the dance, what really matters is being asked onto the dance floor.

When organizations strengthen employees' connections, not only to their mission and purpose but also to each other, they create cohesion. Cohesiveness drives better performance because teams are better able to collaborate. They see how each individual and the team as a whole contribute toward a shared purpose. Unity reduces potential conflict around differing opinions because when we are working well together, such disagreements become fuel for brainstorming and creative problem-solving rather than a source of divisiveness.

Besides diversity, inclusion, and belonging, there is another vital component: equity. Equity means impartiality and fairness. It means that everyone is given the same opportunity. That requires systemic, structural approaches to everything from hiring to team leadership, compensation, and—of course—promotion and assignments to challenging projects. In an equitable work environment, each individual has an equal shot at doing important work, learning new skills, taking on new projects, stepping up to challenges, and succeeding.

Questions to Consider and Discuss

How good a job is your organization doing creating a sense of belonging across all employees? Here are some questions you might want to ask in leadership meetings, in surveys, or at focus groups. These are also excellent discussion topics during employee affinity meetings. (Sometimes called employee resource groups, they have been mainstays of many organizations to help recruit, develop, and retain diverse candidates.)

- Do employees who come from unrepresented groups celebrate and share their differences (whether racial, cultural, ethnic, gender, sexual preference, or something else) or do they try to conceal them?

- Do leaders respect cultural differences, or do they suggest to employees that they need to try harder to fit in?

- Are employees welcome to express their differences in a positive and meaningful way?

- Do leaders open up and discuss their own personal differences?

- Are there unwritten rules about power or prestige (like where you went to school or the kind of degree you have) at your organization?

- Do engagement and other surveys ask employees questions about their sense of belonging?

- Are cross-functional, diverse teams frequently used to solve problems?

- Are offices designed to encourage social interaction?

- Are remote teams given enough attention to feel included in company events and activities?

Discussion of these issues is important, but there needs to be more. The DDI survey mentioned earlier found that it is rare for companies to follow through on diversity and inclusion initiatives. Fewer than one in four leaders agreed that their organizations recruit and promote from a diverse talent pool, and only 27 percent felt that inclusion was a strong part of their company's culture and values. Without such focus, even if diverse candidates are recruited, it is difficult to retain them.

Another perspective on the value of diversity and inclusion comes from the Fortune "100 Best Companies to Work For" list in which

35 percent of leaders from the best companies say inclusion is a strong component of their culture and values as compared with 20 percent of the leaders of other companies.[47] But think about that: 35 percent is not very high at all. There is significant room for improvement.

Unconscious Bias

Blind spots—and we all have them—are difficult to grasp because we are blind to them. They affect who we hire, how we lead a team, and how we expect the world to work. It is important for leaders to examine their own biases if they wish to take diversity, inclusion, belonging, and equity into consideration. These are some common biases to reflect on and honestly discuss with your colleagues:

- Anchoring/Focalism Effect: The tendency to pay more attention to and give more credit to the first and last pieces of information we are offered. This sets up bias against other information we receive.

- Attribution Bias: The tendency to be self-serving and find contextual excuses for our own failures but attribute the mistakes of others to character flaws.

- Backfire Effect: The tendency to strengthen a belief if someone challenges our belief, even if we are faced with evidence to the contrary.

- Prototype Bias: Assuming a person is ideal for a role or task (or is not suited for the role) based on a part of their identity or a generalization about them.

- Similarity Effect/In-Group Bias: Favoring those who share your identity or background.

Diversity Gaps

During the pandemic, between the job losses that disproportionately affected Black and Latina women and the childcare burdens that fell much more heavily on mothers than on fathers, almost 2.2 million women stopped working or looking for work between February and October of 2020 according to the National Women's Law Center. By October, women had only regained 43.9 percent of these jobs. It will take years for these women to fully return to the workforce, and even then, they will experience suppressed wages and lost opportunities.[48]

Globally, 28 percent of managerial positions are held by women, which is almost the same as in 1995, and 18 percent of CEO positions are held by women. Among Fortune 500 companies, only 7.4 percent of CEOs are female. This is an improvement since 1998, when there was only one woman in a CEO role. Further, 68 percent of C-suite level executives are white men, and only 4 percent are women of color. Earning power is also problematic, with Black, Native American, and Latina women earning 25 percent less than White men.[49]

Leaders from diverse groups help organizations build diverse talent pipelines by attracting younger talent who want to work in such environments and by coaching and mentoring current employees who have leadership potential. Put simply, the fewer leaders from diverse groups an organization currently has, the fewer they will have going forward. But hiring for diversity is not enough. Companies must also pay attention to and develop robust retention strategies. According to DDI, senior-level minority leaders are more than twice as likely to leave as their nonminority peers.

In addition, organizations struggle to build a diverse bench of high potential employees. DDI's research found that even in high performing organizations, only 24 percent of high potential leaders are female and only 19 percent are from diverse racial/ethnic backgrounds. Women report that they receive less coaching and feedback than men when they are promoted and are less likely to undergo formal assessments or receive training. That represents a big challenge for organizations. The reality is that 45 percent of women leave their organizations to advance in contrast with 32 percent of male executives. At Ideal Outcomes, we have found that one way to overcome this challenge is to provide regular, formal executive one-on-one coaching for high potential women.

Ensure Your Own Diversity

Diversity matters. We have highlighted multiple examples of how diversity and inclusion drive financial performance. Executives should also consider the diversity of their own professional networks. When your network is more diverse, you gain access to people who think differently and can provide fresh and varying perspectives on how to solve problems and advance your organization.

Examine the organizations with which you currently network. How diverse are they? Seek out associations and networking groups that represent your industry and focus on a diverse membership. Also look at organizations outside of your industry and/or that emphasize a cross-industry perspective. Reach out to the diverse members of your own team and connect into their networks. If you tout diversity, you also must live it.

Take Advantage of Increased Remote Work

Remote work levels the playing field for recruitment and for employees. When organizations are no longer tied to a geographic site for hiring, they can more rigorously go after a more varied pool of candidates. Hiring managers are less likely to subconsciously or consciously reject candidates for discriminatory reasons when they do not see them face-to-face early in the process. People with disabilities benefit from new technologies and remote work, and single parents benefit from flexible work schedules and not having to commute.

Actions That Drive Diversity and Inclusion

There are a number of actions leaders can take to create and sustain a strong diversity and inclusion culture. The starting point is to examine what you currently do to unleash talent at lower levels and from different backgrounds. The right data is critical. Leaders cannot rely on perception or the "feeling" that they are making an effort or driving improvements. A commitment to advance leaders from a diversity of backgrounds is necessary, but as we have seen, commitment is not enough. Take a five-year look back at the following data points and trends for each year:

- Percent of promotions to manager roles versus external hires, broken down by frontline, mid-level, senior, and C-suite managers.

- Average number of promotions for nonminority males, minority males, nonminority females, and minority females. Break this data down by frontline, mid-level, senior, and C-suite managers.

- Year over year, turnover of nonminority males, minority males, nonminority females, minority females. Also break this data down by frontline, mid-level, senior, and C-suite managers.

Once you know how you are performing in these categories, you can develop strategies and action plans to address gaps and shortfalls. The most effective strategies include the following:

- Make investments in employee well-being, including flexible work options that especially support employees with young children as well as those with aging parents or chronic health conditions.

- Clearly define the competencies expected from leaders at all levels, and use this framework to structure formal training and development programs.

- Ensure that every high potential employee has a robust development plan with specific on-the-job experiences and rotations, competencies, and technical skills that are to be addressed, along with timeframes, results expected, and accountabilities.

- Develop mentorship programs. Encourage your leaders to be mentors and sponsors. Mentors help employees evaluate their careers and the skills they need to develop, and sponsors help them make it happen.

- Ensure that next-level leaders have the coaching skills needed to grow talent.

- Ensure that you have fair and transparent performance management systems throughout your organization. Again, look at your data. Do certain managers consistently rate women or minorities lower than their white male peers? Are women and minorities generally rated lower regardless of who the manager is?

- Develop formal transition/onboarding programs for promoted employees to ensure smoother transitions. (The employees who report to them will benefit as well.)

- Use formal assessment tools for all employees to ensure development is targeted precisely toward their strengths and weaknesses.

- Develop retention strategies, taking the needs of women and minorities into special consideration since they are the greatest flight risk. If your minority hires leave, find out why they felt they no longer belonged at your organization.

- Rethink your recruiting processes. Most organizations hire many employees from employee referrals, and with good reason. They often lead to a higher quality of hire. But if your workforce is not as diverse as you want, you are probably reinforcing those numbers because people typically refer people who are like them. Work with human resources to expand sourcing strategies to attract a more diverse workforce.

Strength in Diversity

There is ample data on the power and impact that diversity has on organizational success. If organizations wish to benefit from the value that diversity provides, they must continue to evolve and develop this concept and the purposeful efforts they make. People with different backgrounds will analyze problems differently and arrive at different solutions, increasing the chances of positive outcomes.

Also note that you can't hire someone from a company with a stellar reputation for its culture of diversity and expect them to inject your company with a shot of that culture. The right culture for your organization comes from within and needs to be promoted and lived from the top. As with any business strategy, leaders have to map out the road to success, set forth specific measurable goals, and establish accountability.

Consider Nasdaq's actions in March 2021 after a six-month analysis found that more than 75 percent of its listed companies did not meet its proposed diversity requirements. Nasdaq asked the Securities and Exchange Commission for permission to adopt a new requirement that companies listed on its main US stock exchange have at least one female director and one underrepresented or LBGTQ director and that they report data on boardroom diversity.

If companies don't comply, they would face potential delisting, reports the *New York Times'* DealBook newsletter. This was the first time a major stock exchange demanded more disclosure than the law requires. Companies that report their data but don't meet the diversity standards would have to publicly explain why—and have good reasons.[50]

The bottom line is that any organization must embrace diversity throughout its ranks if it wants to attract and retain new talent for long-term success. Diversity may be the right thing to do morally and politically, but it's also the right and smart thing to do from a business perspective.

7

Become a Culture and Talent Champion

"You gotta build a team that is so talented, they almost make you uncomfortable."
—Brian Chesky, CEO of Airbnb

Fourteen Months

Our CEO's latest video message was amazing. I know our company suffered a significant financial setback last year and we're just starting to recoup losses. Revenue is up, but it's still not where it was before the pandemic. Despite that, he described major investments in people development. What I really liked was the emphasis on cross-department training and development. I learned how valuable collaboration is when we partnered with the Seattle team to create some great customer delivery training.

Our CEO also had our VP of HR describe what will be rolled out in terms of a new learning system platform and said they're shopping for a learning and development vendor to support our leadership development goals. He point-blank stated we don't promote enough people from within and that we don't have the level of diversity we should to support the markets we serve. How many CEOs are willing to admit that!

I was really impressed—and excited. I'm one of a few managers who are women of color in this company, and I honestly feel my career opportunities just took off.

COVID-19's impact on talent was massive. Layoffs, furloughs, and widespread unemployment, as painful as they sound, merely scratched the surface. Companies had to quickly reassess their hiring practices and figure out how to bring new workers on board, often remotely, and if not remotely, safely. Many companies quickly discovered how ill-equipped they were to support remote work from a technical standpoint. Managers struggled to supervise remote teams and employees struggled with a totally new level of work-life balance challenges. Stress and burnout reached new heights.

Secretary-General of the United Nations António Guterres stated, "The world of work cannot and should not look the same after this crisis." Slack cofounder and CEO Stewart Butterfield gave this realistic assessment: "We all know that work will never be the same, even if we don't yet know all the ways in which it will be different." He makes a valid and compelling assessment, but it does not tell us what we should be doing or how to go about moving our organizations forward.

Further, at the risk of sounding like doomsayers, there is a likelihood that other crises will confront businesses, and like COVID-19, they won't be easy to solve. According to the World Economic Forum's "The Global Risks Report 2021," the high-impact risks of the next decade will be infectious disease, climate action failure, weapons of mass destruction, livelihood and debt crises, and IT infrastructure breakdown. Their survey also stated that economic fragility and societal divisions are likely to increase in part due to underlying disparities in healthcare, education, financial stability, and technology in certain groups and countries. Their main concern is that organizations will focus on the last crisis rather than anticipating the next.[51]

There are two core strategies organizations must embrace to recover from the pandemic's impact and to prepare for the next unforeseen crisis. They must embrace technology as part of strategic planning. They also must reinvent their culture, including the talent strategies and practices that dovetail with the company's culture. We are not technology gurus, so our concentration is on culture and talent, which we firmly believe senior leaders need to develop and drive for their organizations.

Start with Culture

The National Association of Corporate Directors (NACD) is quite clear about the importance and value of corporate culture. "Corporate culture can no longer be considered as a soft issue by management. Its strength or weakness has a lasting impact on organizational performance and reputation."[52] There is no question that culture is a strategic responsibility, and the executive team has the important role of providing oversight to the organization's culture to ensure its integrity and continuity.

Consider the impact on organizational performance of cultures with weak ethics. CEB (formerly the Corporate Executive Board and a subsidiary of Gartner) found that companies with weak ethical cultures experience ten times more misconduct than companies with strong ethical cultures.[53] The problem is pervasive. In a recent eighteen-month period, more than four hundred business executives and employees, including prominent global CEOs, were accused of misconduct, including sexual harassment.

Focusing on culture is much more than another form of risk mitigation because culture drives bottom-line success or failure. Investors, regulators, customers, and prospective employees make critical decisions based on their scrutiny of your organizational culture.

In high-performing organizations, the CEO and the C-suite are on the front line, setting the company's culture, although they need input from all levels of employees. We find that the most effective approach is for leaders to take the entire organization into account—from the skill sets of frontline staff right on through to leadership capacity—identifying culture influencers and equipping them to lead down-to-earth conversations with colleagues. Leaders also need to model the desired culture, enforce the alignment of strategies and policies with stated values, and make discussion of culture issues a priority at every meeting. Executives should partner with each other to clearly establish the values and behaviors that will help the company excel and communicate behaviors for which there is zero tolerance.

Another way executives can increase their involvement with organizational culture is to partner with human resources in holding the next level of leaders accountable for measuring culture, reporting on it, developing action plans, and ensuring such plans are executed. Keep in mind, though, that involvement at the top is not enough. While many executives understand the health of their organization culture at the senior level, they have minimal understanding of it at lower levels. Relationships need to be built across multiple functional teams (such as human resources, risk management, and customer service) to increase cultural dynamics throughout the company.

Understand Your Intangible Assets

State Street Global Advisors (SSGA), the world's third largest asset manager, has recognized corporate culture "as one of the many, growing intangible value drivers that affect a company's ability to execute its long-term strategy."[54]

There is no greater indicator of business strategy and priority than the corporate budget, and as we have mentioned, training and development is often the first place organizations cut funding. To drive cultural transformation, organizations must also prioritize talent in terms of budget, dollars, and time.

A key to executive involvement in talent is to increase its understanding of the value of intangible assets. Top Ernst and Young Global Limited (EY) executives Steve W. Klemash, Bridget Neill, and Jamie C. Smith, found that a company's intangible assets, which include human capital and culture, are now estimated to comprise on average 52 percent of a company's market value.[55]

The SEC, along with other groups, is driving efforts to introduce ways in which companies can better incorporate measurement of the value of human capital into financial reporting. The International Organization for Standardization (ISO) has specified twenty-three core human capital metrics for organizations to track and report on including the cost of human capital initiatives and worker productivity, health and well-being, and leadership trust. Core areas include diversity, leadership, culture and recruiting, among others.[56]

Boards, too, are shifting the way they view human capital management efforts as evidenced in the landscape of proxy disclosures. Initiatives include workforce diversity (50 percent), workforce compensation (34 percent), and at 22 percent each, culture initiatives, workforce health and safety, and workforce skills and capabilities. Unfortunately, few key performance indicators (KPIs) are associated with such efforts.[57]

There was widespread loss of jobs during the pandemic. The International Labour Organization reported that in June 2020, 93 percent of the world's workers lived in countries with workplace closure measures. They also estimated that the number of hours worked globally declined 14 percent in the second quarter, an equivalent of four hundred million full-time jobs. While there were sixteen million people unemployed in the US in July 2020, numerous organizations demonstrated the value they place on human capital. Rather than eliminate jobs, they cut pay—including for the C-suite—and instituted furloughs.

As organizations slowly recover from the economic impact of the pandemic, they need to think very differently about how human capital is valued, and therefore treated. The C-suite needs to lead this shift for it to be effective and sustained.

BlackRock, Inc. began to include human capital management as an engagement priority in 2018. It states that a company's approach in this area is a factor contributing to business continuity and success, "particularly in today's talent constrained environment and in light of evolving labor market trends."[58]

If an organization does not have the right people, it will fail to reach its potential. Talent is a crucial competitive differentiator. Executive involvement is essential for organizations to have powerful talent management strategies and practices. Here are some fundamental actions executives can take to move their organizations in the right direction and to monitor progress.

Ensure Talent Can Deliver Value for Shareholders

Talent is expensive. According to Paycor, labor costs can account for as much as 70 percent of total business costs.[59] Executives must embrace the concept of talent as an asset to grow and develop rather than merely a cost to be controlled. Expand your perspective on talent development. Winning companies recognize that talent enhancement is a daily responsibility. That is not to say that costs should be ignored. Analyze your investments in talent and ask for measurements of value returned. For example, are internal promotions increasing? Is turnover of talented employees decreasing? Are net promoter/customer satisfaction scores improving?

Unfortunately, most learning and development programs produce incremental gains (at best) rather than transforming capability. French automaker, Renault, serves as an example of how to rethink talent development with its launch of a multi-billion-dollar comprehensive digital transformation strategy. The CIO and the executive vice president of human resources partnered closely to implement an integrated culture shift across the organization with the goal of putting "digital" front and center in their employees' minds and daily routines. They concentrated on building employee digital skills, including agile methodology.

Managers at Renault had to learn how to be more collaborative. They repositioned their employee branding with a new motto: "Move the world forward." And they made a thoughtful renewal of their core values to align with a digital culture. They also defined ways to move from a traditionally structured organization with its emphasis on individual performance to one with an emphasis on collective performance, keeping the whole company in mind.[60]

Monitor Talent Risk and Increase Management Accountability for Talent

Talent reviews are essential tools to effectively monitor talent risk and ensure management accountability. You can equate the concept of succession planning with building a high performing football team. While there are eleven players on the field at a given time, there are many more players on the team—fifty-three on the roster and forty-six dressed for the game. If the team only builds backup plans for its quarterback, it will be ill-equipped to respond to injuries or other unexpected causes of talent gaps. Consider what your organization needs to do to win. What happens if a central player is out? See talent gaps for what they are: risks to organizational success.

This means having a different perspective on succession planning. It is not enough to identify readiness for the C-suite. There needs to be a succession plan for additional levels, at least down to the manager level. In flatter organizations, this may mean a succession plan for team leads. Also consider succession planning for mission-critical roles, which will vary depending on your organization and, for example, might include software engineers, customer service leads, or account executives.

Make sure your organization evaluates and develops skill and competency-based strategies—not only the skills required today but also those needed to meet long-term strategies. Typically, skills are needed cross-functionally and include the ability to be innovative, agile, analytical, collaborative, and technologically savvy. Know your gaps and develop plans to close them.

In other words, solid succession planning and talent reviews are not enough. When employees with potential are identified, the next step is to create plans to develop them, which is where manager accountability comes into play. Make sure your managers are talent leaders who develop and prepare their employees for new opportunities. Such managers will ignite your culture and should be recognized and rewarded for creating return on your talent assets. Remember that rewards do not need to be monetary. Managers who develop talent should be targeted for greater career growth opportunities, increased spans of influence, and recognition as role models for the company as a whole.

Rethink Compensation

A critical role of executives is to guide the organization toward greater long-term, strategic thinking. Unfortunately, pay does not often align with desired behavior. Investigate ways to balance between short-term incentives and long-term ones. Incentives drive ownership thinking and commitment, and they should be tied to business goals to build teamwork and collaboration. Examine your organization's approach to recognition and other intangible rewards, and make sure they are aligned with company values and strategies.

Pay equity is also a strategic consideration, both internally and externally. To effectively recruit and retain employees, an organization must have internal equity, where employees feel they are rewarded fairly based on performance, skills, and other job requirements. Organizations must also ensure external compensation equity with other employers competing for talent in the same labor market. Pay equity is an important consideration, and many organizations are instituting regular pay equity analyses and audits and developing strategies to correct disparities.

The competition cannot replicate your culture or the experience employees have when building their careers. Executive involvement is an important component to drive alignment between your culture and the development of your talent.

Questions Executives Should Ask Regarding Talent Strategy

Executives need to take a thoughtful, systematic approach and ask themselves a series of questions to assess the strength of their talent strategy. Answering these questions will guide you towards a winning outcome.

- How does our talent strategy support our values, business objectives, and capital investments?

- How does our talent strategy support business initiative success? (For example, a new ERP, implementing lean or agile strategies, and/or process improvements.)

- What development was provided to key talent last year? How was it tracked and measured?

- Are there talent committees that should have an executive champion?

- How are shifts in market and labor demographics impacting our talent and therefore our ability to execute on strategy? What are our greatest risks?

- What is our external hire versus internal promotion ratio? What is the success rate for each?

- How do we measure the effectiveness of our onboarding processes?

- How is our social media strategy integrated with our talent acquisition strategy?

- How do we measure engagement in our organization? What trends are we seeing in our employee engagement? Who is accountable for improving engagement?

- What is our undesirable turnover including top performers, high potentials, and those in critical or hard to fill roles?
- What is our turnover in our diverse employee populations?

Leaders need to be actively involved in monitoring, measuring, and championing their organization's culture and talent, and it must be an ongoing effort. Some of the clearest indicators of a healthy culture include low employee turnover, high customer retention and satisfaction, high levels of trust, a sense of teamwork, and a focus on excellence. Leaders create such a culture when they focus on attracting, retaining, and developing their employees. Talent is the lynchpin for success because people are at the core of any organization's success. The right talent leadership will transform every aspect of your organization. Without the right people no product or service, regardless of how good it is, can succeed in the long term.

8

Turn Crisis into Opportunity

"Never let a good crisis go to waste."
—Sir Winston Churchill and others

Eighteen Months

This past year and a half was the toughest time of my career, and no doubt lots of other people also feel that way. Each week—in fact, sometimes each day—brought a new challenge and unbelievable stress. Yet through it all, I have to say, we all learned a lot. I know I'm a better manager and a better leader for it. I have seen so many team members rise to the challenges and come up with new ideas we never dreamed of.

In some ways, we had it lucky. Many of us were able to work from home. Sure, that had its bumps and adjustments, but we were safe. Many of my friends and neighbors didn't have that luxury. Still, I'm amazed by how flexible our team and our company became, and so quickly. We took care of our customers, many of whom were also hurting, and built whole new ways of working together across the country.

My family came together too. I'm so proud of my husband. And I'm proud of my kids too. They stuck to their school routines, at least most of the time, and although they didn't like remote learning, they did their work and did it well.

After this, I think we can face anything together.

What good can come of a pandemic that claimed so many lives and caused such widespread business disruption? Perhaps you think it's strange to even have a chapter trumpeting benefits from such a cataclysmic event. While that's entirely understandable, there are a number of positive outcomes that will help us step into the future in a better position and with greater confidence.

First, we can learn some lessons from history. The world has experienced devastating plagues before. They didn't stop great advances in the arts and sciences and maybe even enabled them. William Shakespeare wrote some of his most famous plays—*King Lear, Macbeth,* and *Antony and Cleopatra*—locked down in quarantine when the bubonic plague gripped England in 1606.

Just sixty years later, after the plague struck again, a young scholar fled the confines of Cambridge University and escaped to his family's country estate. It was there that Isaac Newton reportedly saw the apple fall from the tree and worked on the papers that became his theory of gravity.

Think about other dramatic events over the course of human history. The Black Death that ravaged Europe in the fourteenth century made authorities aware of the importance of public sanitation. The loss of life created a shortage of labor that empowered workers and eventually led to the dissolution of serfdom.

Fast-forward a few centuries. The 1918 flu pandemic that killed as many as fifty million people across the world led to major advances in preventive medicine and a greater expansion of healthcare for the population at large. Pandemics have sparked innovations in vaccines for many conditions including measles, mumps, rubella, malaria, and polio.

Even in the US, the need for strict quarantines goes back as far as the 1790s after a yellow fever epidemic swept through Philadelphia, the country's largest city and temporary capital at the time. In 1798, President John Adams advocated strict nationwide quarantines to stifle epidemics and set up hospitals to look after sick seamen—an act that led to the Public Health Service. Jeanne Abrams, author of *Revolutionary Medicine: The Founding Fathers and Mothers in Sickness and in Health*, says, "The founders' early experience with epidemics led them to realize early on that the government has compelling reasons to shoulder some responsibilities with respect to the health of its citizens."

Government leaders have the primary role to protect the health of its citizens. Corporate leaders not only have the same responsibility for their employees but also have to consider the health of their company's bottom line. Today it's a given that federal, state, and local governments spearhead health initiatives. But the speed at which multiple vaccines were developed and distributed during the most recent pandemic was a textbook example of how public-private partnership (along with the military) can combine to maximize benefits for the entire population.

Our focus is on the way the business world has stepped up to the disruptive challenges of the pandemic and how corporate excellence and even growth have been stimulated as a result.

Disruption Equals Opportunity

A time of disruption can be the best time to implement overdue change. Variations of the saying "Never let a good crisis go to waste" have been attributed to Sir Winston Churchill, Albert Einstein, and Nobel Prize-winning economist Paul Romer, among others.

Regardless of who deserves the credit, the maxim holds true. Adversity can—and should—be turned into opportunity. A crisis situation makes it easier to persuade people who have been resistant to change, and it helps overcome institutional inertia. In normal times, employees have a strong sense of psychological ownership of the status quo, but when a crisis dominates their work and their home lives, they become more persuadable.

For one thing, employees are less likely to resist new processes if they perceive they have to be made as a result of external factors. The sense of urgency that a crisis creates also drives collaborative problem-solving, innovation, and willingness to experiment.

As an example, the spread of the coronavirus gave retailers considering the introduction of contactless payment the ideal opportunity to quickly do so. It also gave companies debating the expansion of remote work policies the perfect excuse to do that. Consider how many restaurants quickly developed processes to support takeout and delivery and how companies developed meal kits for customers to do the final meal preparation at home. Craig Rowley, a Korn Ferry senior client partner and global leader of the firm's consumer practice, tells the story of one client who had planned to implement a curbside pickup program over the course of eighteen months. The pandemic led them to get it going in eighteen days.[61]

There has also been an overall acceleration of online business. Ecommerce was surging before the pandemic, and online sales reached $791.70 billion in 2020—an increase of 32.4 percent over the year before, according to US Commerce Department numbers. It's a trend that continued in 2021. Twenty-five percent of all retail sales are expected to become digital in 2022, a $1 trillion migration from brick-and-mortar stores.[62]

And the forced experience of working online led to collaboration beyond one's own physical office, including working with colleagues internationally. Research shows that companies intend to continue investing in remote collaboration tools, especially video room systems that connect in-office and remote staff.[63]

Those businesses that accelerated the adoption of new ways to work have "produced previously unimagined gains in speed and productivity, even as the very nature of their workforce was trans-formed," said the McKinsey & Company authors of an article about how the pandemic is redefining work. Those changes have included the removal of boundaries, introduction of technology, and decisions being made by those farther down the chain of command. Among other things, those changes have given employees the kind of empowerment that gives HR a broader base of in-house talent to consider for promotions.

Other benefits? "Leaders have seen that truly agile operating models can deliver meaningful business gains. Total clarity on priorities and goals, nimble resource allocation, and reduced handovers can boost productivity by 20 to 40 percent. A genuine customer orientation with fast, iterative feedback cycles can raise customer-satisfaction scores by 30 points. And people working with a clearer purpose and greater autonomy to make decisions will drive up employee-engagement scores."[64]

Many of our clients took advantage of the pandemic to innovate changes to their processes. For example, one client converted hundreds of hours of face-to-face training into online delivery. Because the company was located in a major metropolitan area, this not only allowed them to safely continue mission-critical training, but also saved hours of commuting to the company training center.

Beyond business, there also have been experiences and improvements on a wide-ranging societal level that will stay with us long after the pandemic is history.

Advances in Healthcare and Public Health

While the phenomenal development and implementation of COVID-19 vaccines grabbed all the headlines, there have been other important advances. Consider telehealth. Doctor visits via computer or smart phone were quickly established once the scale of the outbreak became apparent, and their use quickly escalated. According to CDC research, as early as the last week of March 2020, telehealth visits showed a 154 percent increase compared with the same period a year earlier.[65]

At the end of 2020, Wheel, a telehealth company, reported that nearly half of all patients had used some form of telemedicine. That was up from just 10 percent prior to the pandemic. Some 83 percent of patients expected to continue using telehealth. That is a potential shift of $250 billion of US spending to virtual care.[66] Clearly, this is a system that will continue to be used to a greater extent once the pandemic has ended.

The immediate benefits of a shift to telemedicine include expanded access to care, reduced disease exposure for staff and patients, less need for personal protective equipment, and reduced patient demand on facilities. From the patient's standpoint, there are obvious advantages in time saved by not having to drive to a medical office and hang around in a waiting room.

A related trend that's gained momentum is doctor house calls. Through an app and website, market leader Heal, based out of Los Angeles, enables patients to organize a telemedicine or in-home visit with a board-certified doctor. Since its launch in 2014, the company has delivered more than a quarter of a million patient visits, with a remarkable 540 percent increase in 2020. Operating in eleven states and Washington DC, Heal says it has reduced its patients' trips to the emergency room by 71 percent and saved them more than $88 million in healthcare costs. In the process, it picked up a range of awards, including *Inc.'s* Best in Business list, Deloitte Technology Fast 500, and CNBC's Disruptors List.

Not only has COVID-19 impacted healthcare, it has also high-lighted the benefits of frequent handwashing and improved sanitation. This awareness is likely to continue and reap rewards. An article in *Food Safety News* explained that in addition to flattening the curve of the pandemic, improved hygiene practices on a national scale reduces the burdens of influenza, colds, and viral gastrointestinal disease agents such as norovirus, and can also act to limit the spread of some bacterial agents, such as Shigella.[67]

Says *Food Safety News*, "When good hygiene practices become institutionalized, they become part of the culture. These beneficial behaviors are then passed along to our children and pay dividends in better health and longer life for generations to come. These practices, if they are sustained, will also help to control the next round of emerging pathogens that will surely come."

New Perspectives on Work, Community, and Family

The pandemic also showcased the essential roles of frontline healthcare workers and others who kept the wheels of industry turning such as supermarket cashiers, shelf-stackers, and delivery people. Such individuals—mostly lower income workers—were at great risk of exposure but carried on regardless for the common good.

Stay-at-home orders created new opportunities for bonding within families. While you might think that parents working from home combined with kids getting their schooling at home was a recipe for strife, studies have shown the opposite.

In a Harvard Graduate School of Education study, almost 70 percent of dads reported that they felt closer to their kids because of spending more time together at home. Dads and kids shared their feelings more than before.

All of these positives need to be taken into account when we consider how businesses handle the post-pandemic business climate. Management and employees have been tested in ways they never imagined. Lessons have been learned that prepare us to handle any kind of crisis with the knowledge that companies that prove they can adapt are those that have a secure and thriving future.

9

New Opportunities

"Be not afraid of growing slowly, be afraid only of standing still."
—Chinese proverb

Sometime in the Future

That meeting with our VP of Human Resources and our local university might have been one of the most exciting discussions I have had in a long time. Years ago, in my first job, I had to beg my boss to give me some schedule flexibility so I could attend courses that started at 4:00 p.m. It meant leaving work early two days a week to get to class, but if I didn't do that, it was going to take years to finish my degree.

Next month, my entire team will have a schedule that integrates their work schedules with online live classes and a once-a-month cohort meeting at the university. They each have a personalized learning plan that I will map to department projects to reinforce what they're learning in school while providing the needed skills to complete their projects successfully. What is so amazing is how much everyone benefits. My team will be able to finish degrees or certifications. And I'm going back to work on my master's degree, a goal since my first child was born.

The company benefits a ton too. We have problems to solve and projects to work on that each team member will be a part of—while getting college credit! I think this will not only save the company a lot of money but also cut down on potential turnover. Who would want to leave this kind of opportunity?

So where do we go from here? What have we learned from COVID-19—the world's most recent large-scale crisis—that will steer us safely through the next crisis?

How do we prepare so we are not caught flat-footed the next time we experience a major crisis? How do we ensure our teams will respond to the challenge and work as a cohesive unit to confront and overcome whatever obstacles are thrown in our path? What will the future corporate environment look like? Here are some important things we have learned.

- Creative and meaningful disaster planning has to be at the fore.

- The workplace of the future will be a hybrid home-office balance.

- Managers will need to be more empathetic than ever.

- The structure of learning and training will involve adaptive coalitions, on-the-job application, and increased online experiences.

- Living with purpose is a vital employee demand that has numerous employer benefits.

Pulitzer Prize-winning *New York Times* columnist Thomas L. Friedman offers an optimistic take. "The reason the post-pandemic era will be so destructive and creative is that never have more people had access to so many cheap tools of innovation, never have more people had access to high-powered, inexpensive computing, never have more people had access to such cheap credit—virtually free money—to invent new products and services, all as so many big health, social, environmental and economic problems need solving." [68]

Friedman also suggests a likely result—and an explosive one at that. He believes some institutions may disappear and workplaces will not simply change but be transformed. Ditto for the workforce. We're at a pivotal societal inflection point in the way we work and the way we learn, and it's up to senior executives to get their arms around this shakeup. Let's assess where we stand, where we've been, and where we're likely going.

Crisis Planning

Few companies had a crisis management plan in place that could handle the pandemic, and in all likelihood, few have one in place now. Yet the time to prepare for a future crisis is right now, on the heels of the pandemic. As Vibhas Ratanjee, Senior Practice Expert, Organizational and Leadership Development, Gallup, says, "You may not be ready to think about the next catastrophe, not now when the unknowns outnumber the knowns. It might feel like trying to change bald tires while the car is skidding on ice. But a crisis is exactly when CEOs and boards most need what a cohesive executive team offers—strong partnerships, shared vision, and mutual accountability. The best time to disaster-proof a team is before trouble starts, but the second-best is during it."

Crisis planning requires a thorough postmortem of the most recent crisis—preferably with the aid of an independent third party that can provide objectivity—and a plan for preparing for and responding to future threats, unknown though they may be.

It's easy to focus on the day-to-day challenges rather than take time out to plan for an event that might occur years down the road. We slip all too quickly into a focus on immediate issues, and we need to balance that with long-term thinking.

Teamwork and Leadership

Collaboration and teamwork are critical competencies if an organization is to thrive beyond a crisis. Key to thriving is being able to balance transitory or tactical responses with those that drive true transformation. Such balance is achievable when companies bolster their collective strength with diversity and teamwork. CEOs must lead this charge and can only do that when they deeply understand the strengths and weaknesses of each team member so individuals and teams can be deployed in ways that are efficient, effective, and fulfilling to the people involved.

Perhaps of greater importance is for a CEO to understand his or her own strengths and weaknesses so they can become a good leader, not only when times are good but also, and especially, when times are bad. Yet CEOs rarely invest time to reflect on their own strengths and skill gaps. An Egon Zehnder survey of 402 CEOs who together run companies with $2.6 trillion in sales, found that:

- 68 percent admitted that with the benefit of hindsight, they weren't fully prepared for the job,

- 50 percent said driving culture change was more difficult than they'd anticipated, and

- 47 percent admitted that developing their senior leadership team was surprisingly challenging.[69]

The survey respondents said that while they had felt ready for the strategic and business aspects of the position, they fell short when it came to the equally important personal and not as a "fix" or "remediation" but as a strategic solution for growth and transformation. High level skills that can be significantly enhanced though executive coaching include communicating with candor; building genuine relationships with empathy; creating, inspiring, and leading hybrid, diverse teams; and leveraging adaptability and resilience.

The Way We Work

The need for many people to work from home during the pandemic has profoundly affected the way we will work in the future. "Our bias against working from home has been completely exploded," says Dan Spaulding, chief people officer of online real estate portal Zillow.

Hybrid environments and flexibility are here to stay. The most likely outcome is a hybrid approach with an increasing number of people working remotely as compared with pre-pandemic time. Estimates vary about the extent to which work-from-home policies will be adopted. Top market research firm Forrester says that in the future, most companies will employ an "anywhere-plus-office hybrid" model in which more people work outside the office more of the time. The company predicts that the number of employees working remotely will dwindle eventually from pandemic highs to settle, minimally, at 300 percent of pre-pandemic levels.

The Forrester "Predictions 2021" report found that 47 percent of North American managers surveyed during the pandemic anticipate a permanently higher rate of full-time remote employees, and 53 percent of employees say they want to continue to work from home more.[70] As a major portion of the workforce developed the skills and preference for effective remote work, they have come to expect a work-from-anywhere strategy from their company rather than an exception-driven remote work policy.

PwC's second US Remote Work Survey published in January 2021 showed high levels of satisfaction with remote work.[71] Eighty-three percent of employers said it had been successful for their company compared to 73 percent the previous June. Research with our clients finds that the most effective home-office balance is a 50-50 split. Gallup research has provided a similar conclusion. A Bloomberg study found that 29 percent of employees would consider leaving their jobs if their bosses weren't flexible about working from home.

There is work that can only be done on-site, because of compliance requirements, a need to interact with physical objects, a need to interface with customers, or for a variety of other valid reasons.

Brainstorming and creative problem-solving have also proven to be problematic when employees are never face-to-face. Product engineering and lab work also require some people to be physically together while simultaneously collaborating remotely with others. Facebook's Mark Zuckerberg, who estimated that within five to ten years half of his workforce will be remote, said that in general, people are able to work well on projects remotely but added, "Where there's an open question is on the softer stuff: alignment, social bonds, creativity. It's one thing to work efficiently on projects we're already working on. It's another to brainstorm next ideas."

Telecommuting will never completely replace a brick-and-mortar environment because there are many work demands, like those mentioned above, that require a face-to-face environment. But the days of managers assessing performance by watching employees over cubicle walls every day are over.

Courtney Harrison, chief human resources officer at OneLogin Inc., proposes that we could work remotely successfully full-time because we have proven that it is possible during the pandemic. But she adds an important point. "Do we want to? No. Our culture is built around diverse people and diverse office location vibes and that is what makes us who we are and keeps things interesting. We like each other too much to want to be remote all the time."[72]

Logistics for the Hybrid Work Environment

In our view, there will always be the need for personal connection and the kind of spontaneous and stimulating interaction that happens in a physical environment rather than through a computer screen.

This means that the brick-and-mortar workplace needs to be designed to serve as a hub that enables face-to-face and remote collaboration. Essential to this transformation is the right digital architecture, tools, and software. When the pandemic started, many companies were forced into quick remedial solutions. Now it is time to work with technology experts to determine how to strategically move forward digitally. Conference rooms need bigger screens for video conferencing and training, including tools such as interactive whiteboards. Policies about hot-desking and hoteling, which allow workers to select or book a desk when they want to go to the office, need to be quickly developed.

Igniting an Employee-Friendly Culture

The pandemic highlighted that whenever workers have to vacate their offices for lengthy periods of time there are considerable challenges in the transition back to the bricks-and-mortar environment. While the physical logistics were obvious, the psychological safety of employees became apparent. Some employees feared that if they had a choice and elected to become a long-term remote worker, it could put them at a disadvantage professionally. Others were concerned that they could fall out of the loop, fall out of favor with their managers, and lose out on plum assignments. A Korn Ferry survey found that 37 percent believed they would "face retribution" if they opted not to return to the office when it reopened.[73] In our experience, those senior executives who understood the concerns and were extremely thoughtful in the way they introduced post-pandemic work procedures reaped the benefits.

Leaders learned they must foster an environment in which workers are comfortable in the physical workplace itself, whether that is an open office, a factory floor, or a warehouse facility and that the workspace had to be a safe place, which meant, among other things, that it is secure and sanitary.

Going forward, managers also need to consider the potential impact of remote work procedures on employee relationships. In an intriguing study in Microsoft's Human Factors Lab, which began before the pandemic hit, participants wore an EEG device that monitored changes in brainwaves. The brainwave patterns known to be linked with stress and overwork were much higher for workers collaborating remotely than when they were physically together. The study also revealed that if a pair of workers had their first experiences with one another working together remotely, their brain waves suggested it was harder for them to subsequently work together in-person. That wasn't the case with the opposite scenario, and it is something that needs to be carefully considered.

Research conducted at the University of Chicago calculated that across the board, some 37 percent of jobs can be performed remotely. For tech workers, the number was significantly higher—51 percent. But according to Bureau of Labor Statistics, only 2 percent of employees worked from home on a regular basis prior to COVID-19.

Organizations that have been committed to a positive employee experience for several years were best prepared to handle the pandemic. This is because employee experience is holistic and encapsulates everything an employee thinks, feels, sees, and touches in all aspects of the employee life cycle, from recruitment to separation. Companies will need to better understand their cultures and how employees perceive their employee experience. Tools such as pulse and engagement surveys, collaboration technologies, and practices such as flexible remote work policies are important components of a culture that attracts and retains top talent.

The Way We Teach and Learn

Many of the millions of jobs that disappeared during the pandemic won't return, so there is a huge need for retraining. According to the Pew Research Center two-thirds of the jobless have recognized the trend and have seriously considered the need to change their line of work.

The state of Washington has taken a lead in doing something about the demand for upskilling and retraining. It took some of the federal government stimulus money and developed a "Futures for Frontliners" program providing free tuition to grocery store workers, health aides, and other frontline workers toward the opportunity to earn a certificate or an associate degree. The immediate response was overwhelmingly positive with one hundred thousand applications.[74]

The fundamentals of training and learning have changed dramatically and will continue to evolve. Corporations will not only collaborate to a greater extent with colleges and universities but may also *replace* institutions of higher learning

"The strain the pandemic is placing on higher-education institutions will lure big tech companies to continue ramping up their investments in building learning platforms that will offer both challenges and new opportunities for companies to rethink how they prepare their workforce for the future," says Forrester principal analyst David Johnson.[75]

Many skills you possess today are quickly becoming obsolete. The same is true for your employees. Organizations need to find ways to reinvent career pathing and development. Career paths can no longer follow a simple "learn-to-work" trajectory but rather, as Heather E. McGowan, coauthor of *The Adaptation Advantage,* likes to say, it must be a path of "work-learn-work-learn-work-learn." She also says, "Learning is the new pension. It's how you create your future value every day."

In the future, lifelong learning will be done by what Tom Friedman calls "complex adaptive coalitions," while Ravi Kumar, the president of the Indian tech services company Infosys, argues that companies like his, Microsoft, and IBM will partner with different universities and even high schools.[76]

University students will take just-in-time learning courses or do internships at corporate in-house universities, and company employees will take just-in-case humanities courses at the outside universities. Both will be able to "learn, earn and work," at the same time. It's already begun.

The practical real-world experience of remote work and virtual training has shifted corporate mindsets. Going forward, more and more classes will be offered online, knowing that it is a natural fit for some occupations, but not for all. Also, organizations will want to maintain the flexibility to go back and forth between in-person and distance training in case a crisis or catastrophe necessitates it.

A McKinsey global survey of executives confirmed that remote working is here for the long haul. And companies that made serious capital expenditures in digital technology have already reaped the rewards with significantly increased revenue growth. The report added, "The notion of a tipping point for technology adoption or digital disruption isn't new, but the survey data suggest that the COVID-19 crisis is a tipping point of historic proportions—and that more changes will be required as the economic and human situation evolves."[77]

Learning needs to be firmly rooted into your culture. As Sarah Jenson Clayton, who heads up Culture & Change in North America for Korn Ferry, says, "It's a culture reboot—symbolically turning the page on what has been a difficult chapter. We're leaving the past behind us and looking forward to the path ahead. This takes the culture transition from the merely tactical to the inspirational."[78]

Going Forward with Purpose

It's understandable that CEOs working through a crisis—especially one as crippling as a pandemic—may fixate on urgent corporate priorities and the fight for survival. But this shouldn't be done at the expense of purpose, which is essential in the long haul. The real test with purpose is reimagining how it becomes a vital part of your post-pandemic business.

McKinsey research during the pandemic found that people who said they were "living their purpose" at work reported levels of well-being five times higher than those who weren't, and they were four times more likely to report higher engagement levels. There was also a positive correlation between the purposeful living of employees and their company's EBITDA (earnings before interest, taxes, depreciation, and amortization) margin—which is an indicator of overall corporate profitability.

One thing that may be hard for leaders to admit is how often they have taken talented, motivated employees for granted. Employees deserve better, and a focus on organizational and individual purpose must be part of a broader effort to ensure that employees are given the primacy they deserve.

What can leaders do to help ignite purpose? Zappos is a fine example. The company set up a customer service hotline that moved beyond fielding questions about shoes to resolving people's pandemic-related issues. It kept Zappos' customer service reps occupied in a meaningful, psychologically satisfying way—helping people who were struggling.

Purpose needs to be embedded into the entire employee life cycle, including recruiting, onboarding, strengths-based feedback, and performance management. The more you accomplish this, the greater the value you will reap and the more company alignment you will realize.

In many ways, organizations have already fast-forwarded into the future of work, says Deloitte in its "2020 Global Human Capital Trends Report." Lessons learned and actions taken need to be permanent.

The report says, "While moments of crisis can lead to heroic and unprecedented actions, the sustainability of those actions is where the true path towards recovery will begin. That path must be paved not only with good intentions but with meaningful change. Organizations face a choice between returning to a post-COVID world that is simply an enhanced version of yesterday or building one that is a sustainable version of tomorrow. The risk is more than that of falling behind—it's the possibility of never catching up at all."[79]

As we have discussed, COVID-19 will go down in the history books as a once-in-a-century global catastrophe that impacted humanity on many levels. The business disruption was on an unprecedented scale and has served to alert corporate leaders to be better prepared for the next crisis. First and foremost, it showed how companies with a rich, positive culture were resilient and not only survived but thrived. It showed how companies that were agile and reacted promptly reassured their employees and gave them confidence. It showed that an all-hands-on-deck crisis can bring out the best in people leading to creativity and innovation.

The five disciplines we've detailed in this book go a long way toward developing adaptive leadership skills that will ignite your culture and help you navigate any kind of crisis. Inspiring a shared purpose is a powerful way to motivate your teams and move your organization forward. Delivering such inspiration in regular, consistent communication helps develop unbreakable bonds. Building trust and authenticity is the foundation for strong working relationships and collaboration—employees need to know that you walk your talk. Strong performance management gives employees direction while providing inspiring and motivating goals to strive for. Talent development is the greatest investment you can make, proving to people they truly are your most important asset and have a vital long-term role. Diversity and inclusion build belonging, employee loyalty, and talent retention while enhancing innovation and creativity because people from different backgrounds bring different perspectives to the table.

Embrace and live these disciplines and you will forge a company culture that is not only resilient but also thrives in any crisis. Understanding and applying these disciplines will give you the confidence to handle any threat to your business and set you apart from the competition.

Acknowledgments

Culture Ignited was born out of our experiences during the COVID-19 pandemic, a time that tested the resiliency, adaptability, and creativity of organizations, large and small, that all strove to achieve excellence, day in and day out. The book went through numerous iterations, much like companies did as the pandemic and its message evolved and changed.

A big thank you to our colleagues and friends at Ideal Outcomes, Inc. This team weathered the COVID storm, supported each other during challenging circumstances, and consistently performed admirably. Each team member made personal and financial sacrifices to pivot and deliver first-class services for our clients who also, of course, were adapting to the once-in-a-century crisis. Thank you to Jason Bisping, Jennifer Cassidy, Barbara Gold, Sheila McVeigh, Alexis Moran, Laura Nortz, Nicholas Schmitt, and Nikki Vescovi.

The ideas and actions of many of our clients contributed to the development of this book. We want to acknowledge the adaptive leadership displayed by so many of you as we shared this remarkable journey together.

Finally, once again Melanie Mulhall's top-notch editing skills help deliver the final polished product and Nick Schmitt's creative cover and chapter design gave it a striking appearance that stands out on any bookshelf.

Notes

1. From Shock to Coping

[1] "Latest Work-at-Home/Telecommuting/Mobile Work/Remote Work Statistics," https://globalworkplaceanalytics.com/telecommuting-statistics.

[2] "State of Remote Work 2019: How employees across the United States think about working remotely, hybrid and remote team management, meetings, and more." https://www.owllabs.com/state-of-remote-work/2019.

[3] Jared Spataro, "2 years of digital transformation in 2 months," April 30, 2020, https://www.microsoft.com/en-us/microsoft-365/blog/2020/04/30/2-years-digital-transformation-2-months.

[4] Nadine Malek, "Productivity Has Increased During the Pandemic Due to Remote Work," July 21, 2020, https://www.prodoscore.com/blog/productivity-has-increased-during-the-pandemic-due-to-remote-work/.

[5] Raymond J. Keating, "New Gallup Poll on Working Remotely: The Trends and Future of Work," SBE Council, February 16, 2021, https://sbecouncil.org/2021/02/16/new-gallup-poll-on-working-remotely-the-trends-and-future-of-work/.

[6] "US employees spending an extra 3 hours working during the COVID-19 mandated remote work," March 24, 2020, https://www.martechcube.com/us-employees-spending-an-extra-3-hrs-working-during-covid-19/.

[7] "For Europeans, the Journey to Work Causes More Stress Than Their Actual Jobs (or even the Dentist), New Ford Survey Shows," April 27, 2015, https://media.ford.com/content/fordmedia/feu/en/news/2015/04/27/for-europeans--the-journey-to-work-causes-more-stress-than-their.html.

[8] Lauren C. Howe, Ashley Whillans, and Jochen I. Menges, "How to (Actually) Save Time When You're Working Remotely," *Harvard*

Business Review, August 24, 2020, https://hbr.org/2020/08/how-to-actually-save-time-when-youre-working-remotely.

[9] "Remote Working Cybersecurity Checklist," Cyber Management Alliance, https://www.cm-alliance.com/en-gb/remote-working-cybersecurity-checklist.

[10] Jennifer Moss, "All the Lonely People: Loneliness and isolation in the workplace hurt employee health and well-being—and the bottom line," SHRM, July 20, 2019, https://www.shrm.org/hr-today/news/all-things-work/pages/all-the-lonely-people.aspx.

[11] Megan Cerullo, "Most Americans check in at work even while on vacation, LinkedIn survey shows," July 10, 2019, https://www.cbsnews.com/news/most-americans-check-work-email-while-on-vacation-linkedin-survey/.

[12] Alana Semuels, "The Coronavirus Is Making Us See That It's Hard to Make Remote Work Actually Work," Time, March 13, 2021, https://time.com/5801882/coronavirus-spatial-remote-work/.

2. Inspire and Communicate a Shared Purpose

[13] "Korn Ferry Global Study: Driving Culture Change Key Leadership Priority," Korn Ferry, February 4, 2016, https://www.kornferry.com/about-us/press/korn-ferry-hay-group-global-study-driving-culture-change-key-leadership-priority.

[14] Nate Dvorak and Natasha Jamal, "Maintain and Strengthen Your Culture in Times of Disruption," *Gallup Workplace,* April 13, 2020, https://www.gallup.com/workplace/307931/maintain-strengthen-culture-times-disruption.aspx.

[15] Pam Maharaj and Trevor Page, "The social enterprise at work: Paradox as a path forward," 2020 Deloitte Global Human Capital Trends, https://www2.deloitte.com/cn/en/pages/human-capital/articles/global-human-capital-trends-2020.html.

[16] Gregor Jost, Deepak Mahadevan, David Pralang, and Marcus Sieberer, "How COVID-19 is redefining the next-normal operating model," *McKinsey Quarterly,* December 10, 2020, https://www.mckinsey.com/business-functions/organization/our-insights/how-covid-19-is-redefining-the-next-normal-operating-model.

[17] Tracy Brower, "How To Sustain And Strengthen Company Culture Through The Coronavirus Pandemic," May 25, 2020, https://www.forbes.com/sites/tracybrower/2020/05/25/how-to-sustain-and-strengthen-company-culture-through-the-coronavirus-pandemic/#5181905c3ce9.

3. Build Trust and Authenticity

[18] "2021 Edelman Trust Barometer Reveals a Rampant Infodemic is Fueling Widespread Mistrust of Societal Leaders," January 13, 2021, https://www.edelman.com/trust/2021-trust-barometer/press-release.
[19] Holly Henderson Brower, Scott Wayne Lester, and M. Audrey Korsgaard, "Want Your Employees to Trust You? Show You Trust Them," *Harvard Business Review*, July 5, 2017, ttps://hbr.org/2017/07/want-your-employees-to-trust-you-show-you-trust-them.
[20] Sharon K. Parker, Caroline Knight, and Anita Keller, "Remote Managers Are Having Trust Issues," *Harvard Business Review,* July 30, 2020, https://hbr.org/2020/07/remote-managers-are-having-trust-issues.
[21] Andrea Vrbanac, "Five Ways To Spark Your Company Culture While Working Remotely," August 24, 2020, https://www.forbes.com/sites/forbeshumanresourcescouncil/2020/08/24/five-ways-to-spark-your-company-culture-while-working-remotely/.
[22] Jill Unikel, "How Salesforce Is Continuing To Deliver A World-Class Employee Experience," October 23, 2020, https://www.salesforce.com/news/stories/how-salesforce-is-continuing-to-deliver-a-world-class-employee-experience/.
[23] Claire Hastwell, "6 Tips For Better Communication With Remote Teams," https://www.greatplacetowork.com/resources/blog/7-tips-for-better-communication-with-remote-teams.
[24] Steve Hernandez, "Surviving and thriving – tips for sustaining your organizational culture in a (now) virtual world," *Tampa Bay Business Journal,* October 5, 2020, https://www.bizjournals.com/tampabay/news/2020/10/05/surviving-and-thriving-tips-for-sustaining-your.html.
[25] Hernandez, "Surviving and thriving…".

4. Hone Your Performance Management Skills

[26] Edwin Locke and Gary Latham, "Motivation through Goal Setting," High Performance Institute, February 8, 2018, https://www.highperformanceinstitute.com/blog/motivation-through-goal-setting.

[27] Ben Wigert and Heather Barrett, "Performance Management Must Evolve to Survive COVID-19," *Gallup Workplace,* August 31, 2020, https://www.gallup.com/workplace/318029/performance-management-evolve-survive-covid.aspx.

[28] Kristen Berman, "Why remote work makes people less productive, and what to do about it," *Fast Company,* April 10, 2020, https://www.fastcompany.com/90488625/why-remote-work-makes-people-less-productive-and-what-to-do-about-it.

[29] Wigert and Barrett, "Performance Management Must Evolve…"

5. Build Capability and Develop Your Talent

[30] Sapana Agrawal, Aaron De Smet, Sébastien Lacroix, and Angelika Reich, "To emerge stronger from the COVID-19 crisis, companies should start reskilling their workforces now," May 7, 2020, https://www.mckinsey.com/business-functions/organization/our-insights/to-emerge-stronger-from-the-covid-19-crisis-companies-should-start-reskilling-their-workforces-now.

[31] Becky Frankiewicz and Tomas Chamorro-Premuzic, "The Post-Pandemic Rules of Talent Management," *Harvard Business Review,* October 13, 2020, https://hbr.org/2020/10/the-post-pandemic-rules-of-talent-management.

[32] Pam Maharaj and Trevor Page, "The social enterprise…"

[33] "Amid COVID-19 Vaccine Race, Sabin Vaccine Institute and the Aspen Institute Release Report on Vaccine Hesitancy; A Call to Improve Vaccine Acceptance," June 2, 2020, https://www.aspeninstitute.org/news/press-release/sabin-aspen-report-vaccine-hesitancy/.

[34] Susan Sorenson, "How Employees' Strengths Make Your Company Stronger," *Gallup Workplace,* accessed July 6, 2021, https://www.gallup.com/workplace/231605/employees-strengths-company-stronger.aspx.

[35] David C. Forman, "We Got It Wrong: The Transition from Human to Social Capital," LinkedIn, December 15, 2020, https://www.linkedin.com/pulse/we-got-wrong-transition-from-human-social-capital-david-c-forman/.

[36] Erica Volini, Jeff Schwartz, and David Mallon, "Knowledge management: Creating context for a connected world," *Deloitte Insights,* May 15, 2020, https://www2.deloitte.com/us/en/insights/focus/human-capital-trends/2020/knowledge-management-strategy.html.

[37] Randy Emelo, "Connect to Collaborate," *Diversity Executive,* January/February 2013, https://www.riversoftware.com/wp-content/uploads/wpallimport/files/pdf/Collaborate_DE_Jan13.pdf.

[38] "7 Things You Should Know About Google's g2g Training Method." https://vibons.com/ShowBlog?BlogID=182&Title=7_Things_You_Should_Know_About_Googles_g2g_Training_Method.

[39] Deanna (Lazzaroni) Pate, "The Top Skills Companies Need Most in 2020—And How to Learn Them," LinkedIn Learning, January 13, 2020, https://www.linkedin.com/business/learning/blog/top-skills-and-courses/the-skills-companies-need-most-in-2020and-how-to-learn-them.

[40] "High-Resolution Leadership: A Synthesis of 15,000 Assessments into How Leaders Shape the Business Landscape," https://www.ddiworld.com/research/leadership-skills-research.

6. Create Belonging through Diversity and Inclusion

[41] Thomas Barta, Markus Kleiner, and Tilo Neumann, "Is there a payoff from top-team diversity?" *McKinsey Quarterly,* April 1, 2012, https://www.mckinsey.com/business-functions/organization/our-insights/is-there-a-payoff-from-top-team-diversity.

[42] "Diversity and Inclusion Report 2020," Development Dimensions International, https://www.ddiworld.com/research/inclusion-report.

[43] "CEOs for the future, when the future is now," Korn Ferry, https://infokf.kornferry.com/ceos-for-the-future.html.

[44] "Diversity, Equity, and Inclusion at BCG: Our US Report," BCG, https://www.bcg.com/en-us/about/about-bcg/us-diversity-equity-inclusion-report.

[45] "Diversity and Inclusion Statistics You Must Know in 2020," Sapling, https://www.saplinghr.com/blog/diversity-and-inclusion-statistics-you-must-know-in-2020.

[46] Amelia Lucas, "McDonald's aims to diversify leadership, seeks gender parity by 2030," Today, February 18, 2021, https://www.aol.com/mcdonald-aims-diversify-leadership-seeks-155400959.html.

[47] "100 Best Companies to Work For," *Fortune,* https://fortune.com/best-companies/2020/.

[48] Michele W. Berger, Kristina García, Dee Patel, and Louisa Shepard, "COVID-19 and women in the workforce," *Penn Today,* March 17, 2021, https://penntoday.upenn.edu/news/covid-19-and-women-workforce.

[49] "Diversity and Inclusion Statistics…"

[50] Andrew Ross Sorkin, Jason Karaian, Michael J. de la Merced, Lauren Hirsch and Ephrat Livni, "Nasdaq Pushes for Diversity in the Boardroom," The New York Times "DealBook Newsletter," December 1, 2020, https://www.nytimes.com/2020/12/01/business/dealbook/nasdaq-diversity-boards.html.

7. Become a Culture and Talent Champion

[51] "The Global Risks Report 2021. 16th Edition." World Economic Forum. http://www3.weforum.org/docs/WEF_The_Global_Risks_Report_2021.pdf.

[52] "Report of the NACD Blue Ribbon Commission on Culture as a Corporate Asset," October 2, 2017, National Association of Corporate Directors, https://www.nacdonline.org/insights/publications.cfm?ItemNumber=48252.

[53] "Research Reveals That Integrity Drives Corporate Performance: Companies With Weak Ethical Cultures Experience 10x More Misconduct Than Those With Strong Ones," September 15, 2020, https://www.prnewswire.com/news-releases/research-reveals-that-integrity-drives-corporate-performance-companies-with-weak-ethical-

cultures-experience-10x-more-misconduct-than-those-with-strong-ones-102944724.html.

54 Thomas Fox, "Board and Corporate Culture: SSGS Framework," https://www.jdsupra.com/post/contentViewerEmbed.aspx?fid=35a5ff3 2-75f9-4cb8-92fb-d21192db763d .

55 Jamie Smith and Stephen Klemash,"How and why human capital disclosures are evolving," EY Center for Board Matters, October 29, 2019, https://www.ey.com/en_us/board-matters/how-and-why-human-capital-disclosures-are-evolving.

56 Clare Naden, "New ISO International Standard for human capital reporting," ISO, January 19, 2019, https://www.iso.org/news/ref2357.html.

57 Steve Klemash, Bridget M. Neill, and Jamie C. Smith, "How and Why Human Capital Disclosures are Evolving," Harvard Law School Forum on Corporate Governance, November 15, 2019, https://corpgov.law.harvard.edu/2019/11/15/how-and-why-human-capital-disclosures-are-evolving/.

58 "Our approach to engagement on human capital management," BlackRock, March, 2021, https://www.blackrock.com/corporate/literature/publication/blk-commentary-engagement-on-human-capital.pdf.

59 "The Biggest Cost of Doing Business: A Closer Look at Labor Costs," Paycor, December 24, 2020, https://www.paycor.com/resource-center/articles/the-biggest-cost-of-doing-business-a-closer-look-at-labor-costs/.

60 Stéphanie Mingardon "Digital Transformation from the People Perspective: An Interview with Marie-Françoise Damesin, Executive Vice President for Human Resources, Renault-Nissan-Mitsubishi Alliance," BCG, January 31, 2018, https://www.bcg.com/publications/2018/digital-transformation-people-perspective-interview.

8. Turn Crisis into Opportunity

61 Greg Button, Esther Colwill, Craig Rowley, and Leslie Gordon, "One Year Later: The Harsh Business Lessons," Korn Ferry, https://www.kornferry.com/insights/this-week-in-leadership/one-year-later-covid-impact-on-business.

[62] Joan Verdon, "Adobe: Pandemic Shift Is Permanent, E-Commerce To Hit $1 Trillion In 2022," March 15, 2021, https://www.forbes.com/sites/joanverdon/2021/03/15/adobe-pandemic-shift-is-permanent-e-commerce-to-hit-1-trillion-in-2022/.

[63] Matthew Finnegan, "Businesses to boost collaboration spending in '21 as remote work continues," *Computerworld,* December 28, 2020, https://www.computerworld.com/article/3601992/businesses-to-boost-collaboration-spending-in-21-as-remote-work-continues.html.

[64] Jost, Mahadevan, Pralang, and Sieberer, "How COVID-19 is redefining…"

[65] Koonin LM, Hoots B, Tsang CA, et al. Trends in the Use of Telehealth During the Emergence of the COVID-19 Pandemic — United States, January–March 2020. MMWR Morb Mortal Wkly Rep 2020;69:1595–1599. DOI: http://dx.doi.org/10.15585/mmwr.mm6943a3external icon.

[66] "Master Guide to Telehealth Statistics in 2020," Wheel, December 14, 2020, https://www.wheel.com/companies-blog/master-guide-to-telehealth-statistics-in-2020.

[67] Roy Costa, "Hidden public health benefits of the COVID-19 experience," *Food Safety News,* April 28, 2020, https://www.foodsafety-news.com/2020/04/hidden-public-health-benefits-of-the-covid-19-experience/.

9. New Opportunities

[68] Thomas L. Friedman, "After the Pandemic, a Revolution in Education and Work Awaits," *New York Times,* October 20, 2020, https://www.nytimes.com/2020/10/20/opinion/covid-education-work.html?

[69] Kati Najipoor-Schutte and Dick Patton, "Survey: 68% of CEOs Admit They Weren't Fully Prepared for the Job," *Harvard Business Review,* July 20, 2018, https://hbr.org/2018/07/survey-68-of-ceos-admit-they-werent-prepared-for-the-job?

[70] "Predictions 2021: Accelerating Out Of The crisis." Forrester, https://go.forrester.com/predictions-2021/

[71] "It's time to reimagine where and how work will get done - PwC's US Remote Work Survey," PWC, January 12, 2021, https://www.pwc.com/us/en/library/covid-19/us-remote-work-survey.html.

[72] "Companies reveal their plans for what work will look like when America returns to the office," April 25, 2020, https://www.market-watch.com/story/companies-reveal-their-plans-for-what-work-will-look-like-when-america-returns-to-the-office-2020-04-24.

[73] Ronald Porter, Dan Kaplan, and Mark Royal, "Back to the Office … or Else?" Korn Ferry, https://www.kornferry.com/insights/this-week-in-leadership/back-to-the-office-or-else.

[74] Heather Long, "Millions of jobs probably aren't coming back, even after the pandemic ends," *Washington Post,* February 17, 2021, https://www.washingtonpost.com/road-to-recovery/2021/02/17/unemployed-workers-retraining/.

[75] David Johnson, "Predictions 2021: Remote Work, Automation, And HR Tech Will Flourish," Forrester, October 29, 2020, https://go.forrester.com/blogs/employee-experience-in-2021/.

[76] Friedman, "After the Pandemic…"

[77] "How COVID-19 has pushed companies over the technology tipping point—and transformed business forever," October 5, 2020, McKinsey, https://www.mckinsey.com/business-functions/strategy-and-corporate-finance/our-insights/how-covid-19-has-pushed-companies-over-the-technology-tipping-point-and-transformed-business-forever.

[78] Gary Burnison, "Culture: It's How Things Get Done," Korn Ferry, https://www.kornferry.com/insights/special-edition/how-things-get-done.

[79] "Returning to work in the future of work: Embracing purpose, potential, perspective, and possibility during COVID-19," Deloitte 2020 Global Human Capital Trends Report, https://www2.deloitte.com/us/en/insights/focus/human-capital-trends/2020/covid-19-and-the-future-of-work.html.

About the Authors

Jason R. Richmond

Jason is an authoritative culture change strategist whose work over the past twenty-plus years has helped companies build strong, sustained revenue growth by empowering their employees and developing energizing office cultures.

As President/CEO and Chief Culture Officer for Ideal Outcomes, Inc., he has worked closely with established Fortune 100 companies to create Leadership Development Journeys, and he has guided numerous start-ups on the path to become noted industry leaders. He has also provided thought leadership and innovative consulting services to a wide range of midsize companies.

Author of the groundbreaking book *Culture Spark: 5 Steps to Ignite and Sustain Organizational Growth,* and a member of Forbes Business Council, Jason is an in-demand keynote speaker who captivates audiences with his direct, refreshing, no-nonsense style.

An avid traveler, Jason absorbs culture from around the world helping become a valued resource for many organizations in the implementation of talent development paths, culture maps, succession plans, and learning strategies. His experience is matched only by his passion for fostering culture and for helping others grow into leaders. At Ideal Outcomes, he leads a team that guides organizations in creating and sustaining a culture of continuous improvement in which adaptive leadership is a cornerstone.

Jason lives with his wife Julie in Colorado Springs, Colorado. With a passion for healthy living, in his spare time Jason takes advantage of all the outdoor activities on his doorstep.

Jeanne Kerr, SPHR

Jeanne is the Director of Organizational Development and Culture Consulting for Ideal Outcomes, Inc. She also has been a Senior Faculty Partner with the Human Capital Institute since 2012. With over twenty years of organizational development and talent management strategy in a variety of industries, her expertise includes culture strategy, strategic workforce planning, leadership development, team building, and assessment solutions.

Jeanne has her MA degree from Columbia University Teachers College and her BA from SUNY at Stony Brook. She has certifications as a Senior Practitioner in Human Resources (SPHR) and Strategic Workforce Planning (SWP). She is also author of *So You Want a Seat at the Table: A Practical Guide to Being a Strategic Business Partner.* Jeanne lives in Colorado where she takes delight in hiking and cross-country skiing.

Photo by Kennedy A. Johnson

Malcolm J. Nicholl

Malcolm is a former award-winning international journalist whose career includes atwo-year stint as Belfast Bureau Chief for London's *Daily Mirror.*

He has authored or coauthored seven books published in nine languages by international giants such as Random House, Bantam Doubleday Dell, Ballantine Books, and St. Martin's Press.

Malcolm has also ghostwritten more than thirty books specializing in business and entrepreneurship, education, memoir, and health and wellness. He has collaborated with owners of billion-dollar companies and startups, scientists, doctors, nutritionists and academics, and individuals with remarkable life stories.

In a separate career as an entrepreneur, he helped build a billion-dollar business and created innovative marketing concepts combining direct response television and direct sales. A British-born American citizen, Malcolm lives in Del Mar, California with his wife Sandy.

What did you think?

Thank you for reading *Culture Ignited.*
We'd really appreciate your feedback.

Your input will enable us to enhance the services that we offer
to our clients—and our next book. The best way to tell us
what you think is by way of an honest review on Amazon.

A review also helps potential readers decide to get the book!
— *Jason, Jeanne, and Malcolm*

Free Consultation

Jason Richmond offers a complimentary consultation
to qualified organizational leaders.
Please write to us at: *jason@idealoutcomesinc.com*